39054   1/11/10

W9-AYV-377 Ed.

Widow's Journey

Widow's Journey

A Return to the Loving Self

XENIA ROSE

Henry Holt and Company
New York

Published by Henry Holt and Company, Inc.,
115 West 18th Street, New York, New York 10011.
Published in Canada by Fitzhenry & Whiteside Limited,
195 Allstate Parkway, Markham, Ontario L3R 4T8.

LIBRARY OF CONGRESS CATALOGING-IN-PUBLICATION DATA
Rose, Xenia.
Widow's journey : a return to the loving self / Xenia Rose. — 1st ed.
p. cm.
ISBN 0-8050-1193-5
1. Widows—United States—Life skills guides.   2. Widows—United States—
Psychology.   I. Title.
HQ1058.5.U5R67   1990
306.88—dc20   90-32334
                                                                                    CIP

Henry Holt books are available at special discounts for
bulk purchases for sales promotions, premiums,
fund-raising, or educational use. Special editions or book
excerpts can also be created to specification.

For details contact:
Special Sales Director, Henry Holt and Company, Inc.,
115 West 18th Street, New York, New York 10011.

First Edition

Designed by Kathryn Parise

Printed in the United States of America
Recognizing the importance of preserving the written word,
Henry Holt and Company, Inc., by policy, prints all of its
first editions on acid-free paper. ∞

10 9 8 7 6 5 4 3 2 1

Grateful acknowledgment is made for permission to
reprint excerpts from *Necessary Losses* by Judith Viorst,
copyright © 1986 by Judith Viorst.
Reprinted by permission of Simon & Schuster, Inc.

To Warren

Contents

Contents

Acknowledgments

My thanks:

To Pat Bertrand, who, as always, provided me with information, corroboration, and support.

To Ina Torton, who knew that I had to grow in order to make the book grow.

To Cynthia Vartan, my editor at Henry Holt, who asked all the right questions and made me dig for hard answers.

To Robert Markel, who understood and encouraged the writing of this book long before he had a justified reason for doing so.

And my most special appreciation and thanks to the many widows whose unique experiences appear throughout the book. To protect their privacy their names have been changed, but their generosity and willingness to help me and one another needs no protection.

Widow's Journey

1

The Beginning of the End

In May 1984, my husband, Leonard Rose, was hospitalized with acute leukemia, which, six months later to the day, killed him. One of the great cellists of the twentieth century, he was certainly the greatest cello teacher in history. He was also my love and my best friend.

We were married for twenty years. There was never a question on the part of either of us that, given the opportunity to marry each other again, we would not have done so.

Our marriage was never peaceful because neither one of us was a tranquil sort. We thrived together because we had profound respect for each other and mutually accepted the internal devils that we both brought to the marriage. Our individual compulsions and neurotic restlessness was shared territory in which we found the comfort of familiarity.

Leonard loved his life. Maintaining his own flawless artistry was a full-time job in itself, but he also managed many hours of teaching at the Juilliard School in New York City.

He dealt gracefully, always, with the demands of teaching, practicing, and concertizing all over the world, and his legacy of superb young cellists continues to dominate the music scene today.

For the first two years of our marriage, I went with him wherever his career took him. I loved him and I loved his music, and for a while I was content to follow him along as "the wife." Briefly the role felt comfortable—and then it didn't. The physical demands were staggering: the traveling, the late-night concerts, the parties that followed. I was exhausted by the tensions that build around performing, and by "the wife" role, which called for a lot of politicking and meaningless social transactions. People will forever need royalty to worship, so the musical world bowed down to us. After a hard concert, which followed a grueling day of travel and rehearsal, Leonard accepted the public demands upon him with wit and charm. The quintessential performer, he saw these appearances as part of his job. But I soon flunked my part in it. Being treated like royalty began to make me feel totally unconnected and, in time, equally isolated. I was also being worn down by the frenetic pace that serves as a mobilizing force for performers. Passionate and demanding, artists complain and thrive as they build their careers. Their spouses and families, however, tend to become depleted.

It didn't take long for both Leonard and me to realize that there were limits on how much of this life I could handle. It did take me a little time to admit that I wanted something to do that was mine alone, something not connected to his world. It seemed so paradoxical: a few years earlier, I had wanted nothing more than to embrace his life totally and make it mine. Now I was acknowledging something so different that we were both surprised. I don't think Leonard understood exactly what I wanted, or *why* I wanted it, but as always, when it came to my needs, he could accept them without having to understand them. And so now he took for granted my yearning to do something separate. His greatest gift to me was to encourage my pursuit of an old interest: I wanted to be a psychotherapist.

Without his support, I know I could not have pushed myself through graduate school and then through the beginnings of my career. The more I worked, the more interested he became and, despite the limiting of our time together, we both knew we were happier than we had been before. He saw that my job, despite its conflicts and struggles, added to our marriage in a major way.

And then one day this life blew up in our faces. Leonard was dying, and so was our relationship. Overnight we went from being two best friends to two lost people. Every day we grappled with his cancer, his doctors, his hope and despair—each of us desperately trying to hold on to what we had once had. His world became New York Hospital and cancer. Mine was one in which I pretended to cope with everything that went on outside the hospital, all the while trying to stay connected to Leonard. We played the game: endlessly protective of each other's feelings. He wanted to be strong and in total control of his situation, which included a demand for my strength. When I suggested that I stop work so I could spend more time with him, he was adamant that I not even consider the idea. We talked about his illness endlessly, but neither of us could show the other how we really felt. We were two brave, tough, stiff soldiers avoiding at all costs seeing each other in pain. And like two children, we hoped it would go away.

I began to question everything I was doing. I should be with him more. I should be different. Above all, I should be able to make things better. At first I struggled with these feelings, both alone and with my friends, convinced that I could find answers. But the one person who had always helped me find answers was now lost to me forever. So I was forced to find my way as he found his. He remained in control of his world, turning the hospital into a huge stage on which he stayed, to the end, in the center. The nurses and doctors adored him for his quiet courage and strength and his acceptance of this unspeakable tragedy. Famous colleagues came to him from all over the world, bringing gifts and tales of his beloved realm of music. They left filled with admiration for the way he was handling himself.

Periodically there would be bursts of rage. He saved these for me and for his grown daughter from a previous marriage, selecting us to receive his anger because we were not his audience. We were wrestling with death, something for which there was never any resolution; there was no way to win and, even worse, no right way to confront it. I think that in the end we all did the best we could. Leonard died very much in the style in which he had lived: demanding, perfectionistic, controlling, always fair, and above all, possessed of an elegance with people and an unfailing belief in my strength and capacity to survive.

I had reinforced this belief in me, hiding my growing panic and increasing sense of fragility because I knew how important it was for him to believe I was strong and intact.

The night after the funeral I was overwhelmed with feelings—should-haves, should-not-haves, missed opportunities, and endless questions about everything concerning him. Had I found the best medical care possible? Should I have spent more time with him during his illness? Why him? Why me? Why, why, why?

Terrified, I felt lost and helpless—completely ungrounded.

Again friends tried to find answers for me, thinking answers would make me feel better. A month later I discovered that I didn't want answers at all. What I wanted most was to hear that other people felt, or had felt, the way I was feeling, that I wasn't totally alone in what I was going through.

It took me almost a year to find my way. About that time, a colleague, knowing my personal situation, referred a patient to me who had recently been widowed. The patient came to find out if she was the only person in the world who felt totally isolated and utterly confused.

I was way ahead of her. As a year-old widow I realized how far I'd come and how much I knew simply as a result of the year. My new patient described her sense of isolation, her worry that her feelings were "crazy" or "sick," her concern that she couldn't let anyone know about her internal chaos.

How familiar ignorance, fear, self-punishment, confusion, guilt, conflict, even physical problems are—and all so much worse when you think you're alone; yet so many widows can't or won't let people know how these feelings affect them. They stay alone, doubly alone. Having no partner and being in isolation can destroy a person. My patient reminded me of myself despite her being a separate and unique person, a victim of circumstances completely different from mine, yet asking questions and expressing feelings that were similar to the questions I'd had and the feelings I'd expressed immediately after Leonard's death.

A year had passed and I was hearing the language of loss spoken by someone who was convinced she was the only person who spoke and understood its meaning. She was the first person who made me realize that these feelings, questions, and the problems that go with them are universal, and with that realization came the knowledge that we widows are not alone.

I hope this book will emphasize our universality, commonality, and mutuality. It is about my becoming a widow—about Leonard Rose's death and how it changed every aspect of my life, and about feelings I once believed no one could understand. It is also about widows with whom I have worked professionally and others whom I interviewed when I began this book. It is my hope that it shows that no widow is alone in her feelings and that there are ways to make widowhood a little more bearable.

2

Nothing Will Ever Be the Same Again

A New World

Everything is different. *Everything!* There isn't one single transaction that seems even familiar. The world is upside down, somehow, and you're in the middle of great confusion trying to make sense of it all. Actually the world hasn't changed, of course—it's *your* world that has. The places you used to go with your husband, the things you did together, the people you saw socially, all seem changed. The things you once did so easily, without even thinking, may seem to you like major undertakings—hurdles you can't manage.

There are real, not imagined, reasons for these feelings. Don't make the mistake so many of us did: if you're trying to re-create the old world that you miss so much—don't. It's gone, and coming to terms with that reality is very painful. Think about it first as purely an intellectual exercise. Your world was the way it was because it involved both you and your husband. How can your world survive intact when half of what made it has gone? The people, places, activities, the hopes, the dreams, the relationships—everything that made up the old life has changed. You are being forced out of that world and into something else.

The problem is, *what* "something else"? Obviously there has to be a long transitional period while you look for the something else that includes new people and new activities and pushes you into whatever it is that's called a new and different life. If you cling to your old life out of a desire for the familiar, and don't even *try* new and different ways of living, you'll find yourself stuck and very frightened. There is nothing worse than chasing after a dream that you know on some level has gone forever. It's a constant reminder of your loss, and it makes you feel as if the chase is your only option.

I remember longing to be "my old self" again. I wonder now what I meant by that. I know it had to do with wanting to feel better, to feel alive again, maybe even to feel joy. But I think that phrase meant to me, as it may to you, a yearning for the old me in the new life. Every transition creates new parts of people, so why did I fail to realize the profound depth of this transition? Marriage, children, career changes, the death of a parent are all major transitions through which we pass, altering ourselves as we move with various degrees of pleasure or pain, but without a yearning for that "old self." The yearning is symptomatic of a condition that there is no "new self," but only a "present self." And that, for the moment, seems intolerable. No one can tell you now what the new self will be, and you might have to spend years defining it, because the present self, by definition, is time-limited and can nurture itself only with your miserable help.

Misery can keep you stuck and being stuck can make you

miserable. Depression is a formidable force that, uncontested, can destroy. I had two reactions to depression. The first was to embrace it and cling to it as if it were an important friend. I could sit and with little effort utter one word, or think one thought, that by itself could sweep back an entire segment of my past life. One little word, one little memory—and sweet, touching moments were re-created before my tearing eyes.

At first I didn't realize that I was the stimulator for these deeply painful images. Even when I recognized myself as the perpetrator I continued to do it, despite the pain, or because of it. It was my way of holding on to Leonard.

Now I realize that I was afraid to let go. I equated not being miserable with not caring, and not caring was intolerable. A widow told me, "I'm afraid of time. Each day I feel farther away from the life Bob and I had together. I'm afraid I'll forget." The reality is that each day does take us further away from the past. But it's not a question of forgetting or not caring. Paradoxically, letting go allows you to reconnect in a different and healthier way. Time and distance tell you, order you, to redefine yourself. No matter what changes you make, no matter how much you grow, you and your husband will have an ongoing connection. You don't have to ruminate constantly to keep it in place—it is in fact part of you.

Who Are Your Friends and Where Have They Gone?

This is the time in your life when you need friends the most. Your *best* friend is gone, and if there's ever a time when it's essential to feel connected and supported, that time is now.

We've all heard stories about widows who found themselves bereft of friends because they were no longer part of a couple. It's true that many people find the uncoupling of their friends hard to deal with, and often, after a brief "come-to-dinner" period, they stop calling. They're out of practice in dealing with single people and they don't find it comfortable. It's harsh and sad, but there's much that's worse.

First, there's the contagious syndrome. That doesn't sound as if it could ever be displayed by anyone who's educated or informed, but believe me, it occurs even among the intelligent. Whatever disease killed your husband, such people reason, *you* might have it now and could give it to others. These acquaintances disappear immediately and for good. No contact means no catching. Then there's the less concrete version, but the dynamics are the same. You've forced your friends to look life straight in the face and nobody wants to do that. You've showed them that life can blow up in anybody's face, at any time. Even the smug, the safe, the young, and the healthy can have it happen to them. Death is ugly and so is everything that happens after death. People have great difficulty dealing with what's happened to you because it rattles their own sense of security and safety. They too will vanish from your life.

My patient Jill told me of her experience with the contagious syndrome. She and her husband, Harvey, had been longtime friends of Betty and Michael. Shortly after Harvey died, Betty invited Jill to spend the day with her in the country. They had lunch, went for a walk, and chatted happily through most of the afternoon. Then Betty began telling her about a dinner party she and Michael were giving that evening. She went to great lengths to describe it—

naming couples they both knew, the menu, even the wines she was going to serve. Suddenly Jill realized she wasn't being invited. She felt helpless and hurt. How could Betty be so unfeeling? They'd been close friends for years and if Harvey was alive, they would have been included. But of course Jill was not to be included by herself. Jill said, "Betty would no more have told a married friend about a coming party if she wasn't invited to it than she would have flown to the moon!" Jill noted that the incident made her feel like a nonperson.

Another patient, Gail, told me that she had decided the reason she wasn't being invited to parties was that her host and hostess wanted "up" people. "Inviting a widow is kind of like inviting a person with one leg to a party; a downer!" she said.

Still worse are those very close friends who are yours apart from your couple world—friends made through your separate life with your children, or through your work, or through separate interests. We assume they will always be there for us, regardless of transitions and changes, because they are ours. Don't count on it. They held your hand throughout the dying period, but now it's over and perhaps so is their friendship. How can this be?

It's possible that your friends are feeling depleted by your demands. Remember how dependent you've been feeling and acting? You've been accustomed to depending on your husband for many things; now you've transferred this dependency onto everyone and anyone who is willing to accept *it* and *you*.

After Leonard died I was at my most dependent stage. I don't believe any widow can claim to be anything else. Two of my closest friends who had been totally supportive throughout Leonard's illness assumed when it was finally over that I would fall apart and demand constant, endless, narcissistic supplies for my relentless needs. They became less and less available and quickly, quietly vanished.

But they were wrong. I didn't fall apart, and as for my narcissism, which certainly has to be watched carefully at all times, it was under control. Paradoxically, my interest in other people was at an all-time high. I wanted to be involved in other people's interests and lives in a deep and intense way. I'd had enough of myself, my life, my hardships, and my pain. My two friends didn't wait long enough to find this out. When they fled, they left new and raw holes in my life.

Yes, it was grim, but it wasn't the whole picture. There were other people who stayed and negotiated new relationships with me and now continue to be very much a part of my life.

You should look very carefully before you decide anything. You may well find friends who have signed on for life. I did. But because of your present feelings of abandonment and gross inadequacy (a dreadful combination), you may assume no one is out there, and lose really caring people. Give people a chance not to abandon you before you abandon them.

Do you feel you're boring? That's a part of the self-loathing and feeling inadequate. It's also part of something else that's very important: a woman's conviction that it was her husband who was the social bright light, the drawing card that made things work socially. If your husband was attractive, successful, charming, compelling, and all those good things, you are a likely candidate to inherit this problem. Even if he wasn't all those things, you may have thought he was and assumed everyone else did too.

Think carefully. Think about the people you and your

husband knew together and wonder to yourself how they saw and reacted to each of you separately and to the two of you together. Be sure you don't project your feelings onto them. Widows are often astonished to find out that some friends preferred them to their husbands the entire time they were friends. I asked a newly widowed friend with whom Leonard and I had been friends for years why she thought the four of us had been so close. Her vision of her role in the friendship was heartbreakingly comical. She saw the four of us tightly knit together because of her husband's wit and charm and his capacity for friendship. I was staggered. Leonard and I had always talked about *her* charm, *her* sensitivity, and our clear preference for her.

After Leonard died, I was forced to examine my attitude as part of a couple and my feelings about our friends. People who had focused on Leonard and were "his friends" in time became my friends. But only when I let them. On my own, I never would have pursued them, since I never related to them as "my friends." It's enough of a tangle for married couples when everyone's alive. It can be utter confusion when someone dies. My advice is to look at yourself and your husband as a couple and at the same time look at your friends. How were *you* perceived and how were people reacting to *you* without your knowing it? You may find you don't know the answer because you've never asked the question. And you may find people out there whom you've known for years without realizing they could be your friends.

If your only social life was as part of a couple you will have some difficulty with this. Are you ready to deal with yourself as a single person or are you still stuck with the notion that you're only interesting when you're joined to someone else? You can get over these feelings only by trying and testing. Learn to use your telephone. Get off your bed and make a call to a friend with whom you've been out of touch. Be aware that you don't know what the reaction will be at the other end and that you can't predict the outcome. You should also bear in mind that the call is not a commitment for a dinner party. Maybe you used to do that, and perhaps at some later point you will want to again. Right now you're shopping for friends, not proving that you're the best cook in town. You have various options for meeting, including lunch, brunch, in or out. The focus should be the contact, not the food.

And you will need new friends. What you have now is a part of an old life. You'll probably keep a lot of these people in your new life but you'll need additional friends too. Earning someone's friendship is not an easy process, and it usually happens slowly. Making friends under the best of circumstances is a lengthy performance. Friends are the result of caring, involvement, nurturing, and sharing, a process that always takes time. Now you're in a hurry because you're lonely and afraid you can't do it, but you can and you will, as you go about living very much in the same way as you did with your husband. It's similar, but harder because you're doing it by yourself.

Who Am I?

Now the big question is, *Who are you?* This was difficult for me. Without Leonard, I wandered about asking myself, "Who am I? Am I married when I'm a widow? Does my wedding ring mean I'm still married? If it doesn't, what *does* it mean and how do others interpret my wearing it? If I don't wear it, does it mean I'm disloyal? Would I be terminating a marriage that I don't want terminated?"

Suddenly a small thing, a wedding band, assumes major proportions. I've rarely talked to a widow who wasn't struggling or hadn't already struggled with the issue of her wedding ring. Pam, a patient, told me that she would *always* wear the ring because "it makes me feel safe. No man will come near me as long as he thinks I'm married." When we talked about her rationale for wearing her ring, she admitted that it didn't make sense since men made passes at married women as well as at unmarried women. She toyed with her ring, looking at it as if it were a part of her finger. "I've worn it for so long," she said, "if I take it off I'll be a different person."

This conflict has a deeper meaning that goes far beyond wearing or not wearing the ring. Our identity has changed. Are we in the single, married, or divorced world? Gone is the couple, but the marriage doesn't go so quickly. It might sound trivial, but *what do you call yourself?* Are you still Mrs. So-and-So, your husband's name, or Mrs. Your Name? Or just plain Your Name and no Mrs.?

I recall trying to order stationery a few months after Leonard died, feeling as if the decision, once made, would tell me who I was. All I'd have to do was open my stationery box and there I'd be. But what I didn't understand was that there was more than one me in the box—there was Mrs. Leonard Rose, there was also Xenia Rose, and finally there was a plain postcard that had "X" in the upper left-hand corner. It sounds simple now, but at the time I got so bogged down by this major decision that it took me three hours to select the stationery, and having made my decision I called the clerk back later and asked for more time to think about it.

I wanted the stationery to tell me who I was. But it couldn't. I forgot I was in a major transition that, like all transitions, leaves room for changes and different choices. I also forgot that no decision I made would be carved in stone.

A decision about wearing your wedding ring can change; one day you'll want to wear it, the next day not. No one else really cares and in all probability they won't even notice whether or not you're wearing the ring. What matters is the unraveling of your life and your fight to redefine yourself as it unravels.

One of the worst moments for me came six months after I became a widow, and in the most unlikely and extraordinary place. I had joined an aerobics class and was given a form to fill out. I was doing fine until the last question: "Nearest relative in case of accident." Before I married I'd always put down my father's name, then transferred this role to Leonard. Now there I was, standing in a gym in the middle of New York realizing in both concrete and symbolic terms that there was no one who would be responsible for my broken body! Leonard and both my parents were dead. Suddenly I was both an orphan and a widow. My mind went blank. Later, much later, I realized I had made a one-on-one correlation between responsibility and caring. No one was responsible for me but me. But I did have people who cared and would help if I needed it. I had forgotten my friends. My false equation had been "No husband equals no one." I had forgotten that my world had more than one person in it before Leonard died, and it still did!

Then came another blow. VISA shredded my card and said I had ceased to exist. Because I had never established my own account, I now had no credit rating. And because I was a self-employed professional and had no "boss" to

verify my earnings, American Express and MasterCard rejected me!

This is just one more conspiratory indicator that you have
stopped existing. Don't let it happen! Fight back by redefining yourself. As soon as possible establish your own
credit rating by having charge cards in your own name.
Those little plastic cards can do a lot to help reinforce your
true sense of identity—and your feeling of worth.

Incidentally, I took off my own wedding ring when a
patient pointed to it one day and asked me when I was
going to get on with my life.

Who's Really Going to Take Care of You?

If you have children it is likely that you'll be able to mobilize
enough energy to cook and clean and take care of them.
And as long as they need you to do this, you'll continue to
provide the nurturing. But there will come a time when they
don't need it anymore, and then, what about you? The
whole issue of caretaking is of you and for you. Widows
have no difficulty acknowledging their own need to be taken
care of; what they don't acknowledge is their ability to do it
themselves. You start out being taken care of, nurtured by
parents, and then there's the marital mix, in which you do
the nurturing and at the same time have a husband who
nurtures you. This means not only feeding and nursing and
worrying about you, but includes, for most people, gifts,
and special acknowledgments of holidays and birthdays.
Suddenly it's you, alone, taking care of you and buying for

you and worrying about you and wondering if you're up to the job.

The first step is to acknowledge that if you don't do it nobody else will either. If you don't feed yourself and don't take care of yourself then you won't be fed and you won't be taken care of. If you are still in the "I'm not hungry, I don't care what I eat" stage, remember that you're the only one who can move yourself toward a more restorative place. The truth is that you're more than physically hungry. There's this little hole in the middle of your being that makes you feel starved. Eating "normally" usually meant sitting down at a table with someone and carrying on a conversation as you ate. But things have changed. Do you find yourself standing at the kitchen counter eating cold food out of cans or cartons? DON'T DO IT! Sit down at a table and don't eat out of containers. The food you're eating these days is at best eatable but not very good for you and, as a steady diet, probably doesn't supply what you need. When I was eating what I called "take-out garbage," I used the excuse that it was quick and easy and that I didn't want to be bothered. There's some validity to this argument, but in considering it as a life-style, better you learn to be bothered.

Symbolically, not being bothered, or taking the easy route, really is a statement about how you feel about yourself. You're not to be bothered with or about. Why not? Because without your husband you're not worth it. This only adds to the feeling of worthlessness that may pervade your life at this point. Conversely, being bothered (I am not suggesting that you have to do this *every* night) is a step toward meeting your needs and letting yourself know that you're not garbage and that you don't have to eat garbage. It also becomes a health issue. We are more inclined to illness now than we ever were. The statistics about people alone who are not taking care of themselves are awesome. Taking care means eating, exercising, and—even more— doing things that make you feel good or at least better than you did before.

Being bothered can include many things. For example, who is going to buy you a Christmas present now? Friends, children, some of the people who used to. But that special gift—the present that you really didn't need but had been thinking about and wanting, a little extravagant maybe, and definitely not something you'd buy for yourself: your husband bought that present, didn't he? Year after year you had a special, frivolous, extravagant, and, above all, not necessary present. Now what?

Well, you can buy it for yourself *or* you can fall into the trap of saying, "I can't afford it, I don't really need it, I have another one almost like it, and I shouldn't spend the money." If you really *can't* afford it, obviously this becomes the determining factor, but more often than not, you'll find you can afford it but the idea of buying yourself a present, from yourself, is so new and so hard that it may not even enter your head. Think about it. It's more than what it seems. It is an acknowledgment that you can give yourself something you want that is really symbolic of so many other things. It is a statement of your ability to handle money, to figure out what you can and cannot afford, to determine how you really want to spend your money. The most important part of this entire consideration is that you are *worth* a present—a concept that was very clear when someone else was doing it but now has to be sorted out by you for you.

One widow told me, "If it's not a gift *from* someone, I don't want it. It's not the present I want, it's the fact that someone wants to give me a present." That's understand- able to a degree, but now let's take a harder look at the matter. If there are things we actually want but deprive ourselves of, the result is double deprivation. The person who might once have given it to us is gone, and that's a major deprivation—so why add to it? Taking care of you is your job now. If *you* don't, no one else is going to, remember?

One of my patients is a recent widow with whom I debated long and hard over this problem. She wanted a mink coat which her husband had not bought because of its cost. She was never entirely clear about whether they could or could not have afforded it before he died, but now she found she still wanted it and, as a result of his death, that she had more money to spend. She couldn't deal with it for a long time. So many issues were involved: her guilt about having more money as a result of his death, her still wanting something he said she shouldn't have, the endless conflict about what she should and shouldn't spend money on, where she would wear the coat, and ceaseless questioning of her own worth—did she deserve to own a mink coat? As I listened to her over the course of many months, I realized she was struggling with fairly universal conflicts: I had heard all of this many times from married women.

But this widow had to resolve her conflicts for herself. Two differences: she had to take total responsibility for her decision and she would never be able to blame anyone else for it. The other side of that coin was that there was no one she could use to support her doubts and fears. So many of us, when we're married, use our husbands indirectly as controls. We're not honest about it; we don't say, "Help me, I want to do something and I'm scared, so could you talk to me about why I'm scared and whether or not I should really do it?" We don't do it that way. Instead we say, "I'm going to do so-and-so," and then we wait for the "No," which is what we wanted to hear in the first place. I remember the time I suggested to Leonard that I have surgery for the bags developing under my eyes, telling him it would improve my appearance considerably. Then I waited for his reaction. At first he was astonished, then appalled that I would risk surgery for vain and unnecessary reasons. "Stay away from doctors as long as you can and don't even think about such a thing. Besides, you look great as you are," he said, to my great relief. I had been terrified of doctors and hospitals and was hoping to be told exactly what Leonard told me.

Many of us react this way about things that make us grow and change—things that are scary. We do it about anything and everything that makes us feel uncomfortable. But now there's no one with whom to play the game. We have to say yes or no and try it. So what if we make a mistake? It's not a life-or-death matter.

As for the widow and her mink coat, after months of indecision and questioning, she finally went out to buy one. She tried on every mink coat in the store and after selecting the most expensive one, realized with a thud that she really didn't like mink. She decided that what she really wanted was a lynx coat, which turned out to be even more expensive than the mink. By then she had come to terms with the matter and she bought the coat in less than five minutes. The lesson for her, and we've all had to learn it, is that on our own, without a sounding board, we are forced into thinking for ourselves—and sometimes we find out what we actually think.

We also discover what we actually feel. The absence of

our husband's voice has taken the cushioning out of our daily lives. Every decision, every feeling is raw and sharp-edged as we question many of the situations we once took for granted.

When Does "Keeping Busy" Mean "Running on Empty"?

The day ends. If you're working, it's easier because the days are spoken for—dealt with and busy. If you're not working, you must fill both daytime and nighttime. And then of course there are the weekends.

If you have a job to go to, you probably are struggling with the hours between 6:00 P.M. and whatever time you go to bed. It's likely that for a while after you became a widow you found yourself quite busy. People invite widows for dinner. It's done. It's expected. Sometimes they even do it two or three times. This ritual is often followed by the occasional invitation from the wife of the couple for lunch. And then not much more. So what about the evenings? Looking back at my own conduct, and having spoken with many widows since, I see two polarized forms of behavior. My first reaction, which is very common, was to run and run on an empty tank. I couldn't (or wouldn't) acknowledge that I was exhausted and needed simply to rest. I tried to fill every evening until I was so worn out from the sheer demand on my energy that I was ready to drop.

There were two reasons for this behavior. First, I was scared to be alone and face my feelings. Second, I was getting my strokes from people who told me how wonderful I looked and what great shape I was in. Little did I know that by putting up a façade I was paying a price. I didn't understand why people were saying those things. I couldn't see that they were saying them because I was seeing to it that they did. I was presenting myself in a way that made them say it and certainly it looked as if it were true. I hid my pain and then became angry because people couldn't see it.

I was caught in a bind that many widows share. You want to go out, but at the same time you're feeling wretched. The friends with whom you'll be visiting wish you well, but you're aware there's a limit on weeping and wailing. Overt misery (yours or anyone else's) gets to be a bore, and the cruel truth is that people have their own lives to lead and their own problems to contemplate, which quickly become their major interest. Fact: you're allowed a short period of overt depression and then you're supposed to function the way you always did. Fact: you're still connected to your husband. Your friends, although deeply saddened by his absence, have moved along with their lives and are beginning to forget. It hurts a lot, and it makes you feel even more isolated. And here is the bitterest fact of all: if you can't hide your misery, you'd best stay home. If you're fortunate you may have a friend of the moan-and-groan school who will continue to come over and let you go through it for the thousandth time, but if not, close the door and sob your way through the night.

When you're sobbing, at the very least you're feeling and confronting those feelings. When you're busy showing the world how together you are, you're denying those feelings, and little by little cutting yourself off from you. No wonder you feel so isolated.

The other extreme reaction is equally counterproductive and slows down your mourning in its own way. If you take to your bed and disconnect from the world, you have only yourself and your sad empty life to deal with. Your tendency to ruminate and isolate will increase with each day and night because it's you and your thoughts, all alone, with no stimulation or break from the outside world.

Find a middle ground that allows you time and space. Try a combination of too much and too little. You'll probably find that one week you're home every night and the next week you'd kill for a night off. You're likely to find yourself wishing you were out when you're home and wishing you were home when you're out. But that's okay. Remember the times during your marriage when you suffered from similar ambivalent feelings? They're not that new. They just feel different.

As for the weekends, every feeling you've had during the week magically magnifies. My God, it's the weekend, and weekends, we all know, are for families. If you have children, you can focus on them (not guaranteed to be a healthy maneuver) and re-create whatever the old weekend activity was. But recognize that this invites the possibility of touching off the explosion of a land mine. Your children are trying to work through their own feelings of loss and maybe they want to fill those spaces with people other than you. You're likely to find yourself on your own, and need to begin the painful process of finding other people with available time. It's a hard new process of making different friends in a different world. Weekends are like summers, holidays, traveling, sickness, and those black hours before you get up in the morning. This lethal list contains some of the most difficult times widows must face. Each one is a test for the alone.

What we all took for granted in the most practical concrete, unemotional fashion suddenly becomes a major challenge. Why is it that when we were married, a vacation was just a vacation? The considerations were simple: where, how much, and when. And the weekends were nonthreatening, easy times, planned or not planned—they came and went without much thought. We each were part of a pair and together we became the weekend.

And now? I remember in the beginning obsessing about plans for the *next* weekend before this one was even over. The idea of filling two days and three nights was a terrifying prospect. I was in a panic and it took me a long time to figure out why I was so frightened. Something about my aloneness was triggering off my worst fears of abandonment. I was convinced that somehow I couldn't make it alone—much the same way I felt when I was little, and frightened that my mother would leave and never come back. Without really understanding my profound terror, I was in touch with the fear, and my conviction that I couldn't survive on my own. After all, Leonard had been part Mommy, and in fact he wasn't coming back—ever! My dependency on him was fairly well controlled when he was alive. When he died the lid blew off, and all my old, unresolved, terrifying baby stuff got released.

I think this happens a lot. You have to work your way through it slowly, and there are no shortcuts to take. And no limits on pain. The end of a weekend is a good place to stop and take a look, and learn something really important about yourself. The weekend is over. You've been alone for most of it. Most of it has seemed intolerable and yet it's Sunday night and you're okay. You've been alone, you've had some real problems structuring your time but you're safe: there's food to eat, there's a telephone to call people if you need to, there's a door through which you can get in or out. In short, your basic survival needs have been met and you've made it through the weekend on your own. Your survival depends on you, not on Mommy and not on your husband.

I fought this revelation as hard as I could. For, despite my so-called independence and conviction that if I had to I could take care of myself, the reality was that I didn't *want* to, and could happily have lived without this learning experience. That's a piece of the truth, and the other piece of truth is that, having been forced to learn it, I'm glad to know it because it helps me deal with the panic that tends (less and less as time goes by) to attack me. And it can help you with the panic caused by the things on your list of fears. It's no good pretending that you couldn't use some help with these fears. You could, but the reality is that you can manage them because you *have* to. It's much, much harder, but harder doesn't mean you can't.

Holidays almost always appear near the top of the fear list. How to get through Thanksgiving, Christmas, New Year's Eve—all the celebrations that were so joyful in the past. So much depends on what you did before and how you feel about it now. If the tradition of holidays still works for you and your family, there's no reason to change it, but so many widows find that it no longer works because it's so different. Don't keep doing something that's uncomfortable just because you used to do it. Above all, remember that you don't have to do anything again and again just because you've always done it before.

For example, if your children are used to coming to your house to celebrate a holiday, it can be turned around so that you go to their house. Or maybe a bigger change is called for. Switch *everything* around; you don't have to do the same thing every holiday. Let your friends know you're flexible. If they think you're locked into a traditional Christmas, for instance, they aren't likely to include you or your children in their plans. And remember, there are other people in the world going through changes, maybe for different reasons, but they may also be trying to figure out what to do with themselves on a holiday and might love to share it with you.

I know all this activity and exploration takes time to work out, and you should know before you try that there's the possibility that you'll fall flat on your face while you're doing it. You could find yourself in places you don't want to be with people you hope never to see again. But I can't recall learning something worth knowing without first falling on my face, so why should this be different either for me or for you?

Questions without Answers

Who makes the decision about what to tell someone who is dying? Should you tell the truth or should you lie? Which is better? People feel adamant about this subject and endlessly argue the pros and cons as if there were a definitive answer.

I wish there were. In my case, and many others, especially when there is a long illness, the doctors are the ones making the decisions, demanding collusion by insisting on lies of silence—using the terrifying threat that to acknowledge reality would guarantee an earlier and more certain death. "Tell him the truth and he will lose hope, and without hope he'll give up and die." That's direct, and the fear it causes assures our compliance.

The most critical event in our marriage is seen from two opposite awarenesses. The doctors lie, and you lie. So you become increasingly isolated from the most important person in your life. Two people who have shared everything are suddenly disconnected by a barrier of lies.

I was split in two; part of me desperately wanted to tell Leonard the truth so we could reconnect, the other part wanted only to protect Leonard from the pain of knowing. I didn't want him to give up, and yet, since I had been told that there was no chance he could improve, why should he have to struggle? But what if the doctors were wrong? I silently swung from one stance to another. At first I decided to go along with the doctors. I lied. Leonard and I chose our respective roles: I was to look pretty and appear highly functional, concerned, and very supportive. He chose to be supercontrolled, very positive, and basically out of touch with anyone who was really important in his life. Only after Leonard was transferred to a second hospital, where a doctor was appalled to learn about the secrets—the lies and the lack of any human sharing of this disaster—did I begin to question the process of dying in isolation. Was I denying Leonard the opportunity to talk about his fear of dying by denying that he was, in fact, going to die?

Today I still have questions without answers because despite the change in hospitals and the attempt to come to terms with what was actually happening, and its final resolution, I'm still not sure if there is a right or wrong. The debate goes on about what should and should not be said. The important thing for us, the survivors, is not to do what so many of us have done—make ourselves our own victims. Every widow I've ever talked with feels, after it's over, that "I should have done more," particularly in this matter of keeping silent. We think back to the lost opportunities to cry together, to hold each other, to be miserable together—to scream and yell together at the injustice of it all. We lost time and opportunities for closeness because of those hospital lies and it hurts—a lot.

But there is one thing we survivors should remember: we

didn't make this decision entirely on our own. Nor can the doctors be totally blamed. There was someone else in this hospital system who was making some decisions for himself. There was a man who was trying to handle what was happening to him in his way: not your way and not my way. He was seeing what he was able to see and dealing with it in whatever manner he could. He was finding his way little by little, and leaving you to find yours. The truth is that despite the guilt, the missed opportunities, and the haunting pain you are now blaming on yourself, you and he entered into an unspoken contract somewhere early on in his illness. It wasn't the first time you made silent contracts. Unfortunately it was the last.

And I believe that were we—with all the insight time brings—to face these issues again, we would resolve them anew pretty much as we did before, mostly because of this silent contract and the hidden decisions that were so much a part of the relationship long before its end.

3

Still Counting the Losses

Where Has My Mirror Gone?

I prided myself on being an independent person, having struggled for years with issues of separation and identity. First I fought with my mother for initiative and elbow room—for my own life. Then I thought I would have to fight with Leonard to maintain my identity in a world in which being married to a star meant you didn't need a self of your own. My mother had wanted me to be her alter ego, and the tinsel world in which Leonard and I traveled never questioned a wife's need to be anything.

Fortunately for both of us, Leonard recognized my need to affirm my identity. He knew we would have to make compromises with each other; after all, two different people were now married and would have to negotiate their independent selves into a couple, a pair with a couple identity. This couple identity was much more than an attachment; it became a source of self-identification and self-worth. We became each other's mirrors. Our identities were being re-defined by our mutual roles, by our increasingly gratifying interactions and, above all, by the reinforcement of our competence.

My sense of self, to a great extent, became linked to being Leonard's wife as his sense of self became linked to his marriage to me. We reassured, validated, reinforced, and encouraged. We mirrored the best of each other. I lost that mirror when Leonard died. It was a double death. When he had said, "You're wonderful," I believed him because of the interaction between us. At other times he had been critical, and was right to be so, and I managed to change because of him. Now I wasn't sure.

I had had a way of being socially snooty to the sycophants of the music world who hung on Leonard's every word, the kind who attend gatherings determined to wedge themselves immediately into the presence of the "star"—and cling! My haughty reaction was to freeze them out in order to make room for the real friends. But as Leonard said, my nastiness only served to isolate me and, as he predicted, my learning to be an agreeable part of the group did me more good than I could have imagined. Behaving as master cellist Leonard Rose's wife *should* behave—with social evenhandedness—reinforced our couple identity.

But with Leonard gone, I felt paralyzed. It was as if he had taken a major part of me with him. I also felt the loss of a mirror in very concrete ways. I had always been able to dress in five minutes, but now I was anxious and unsure. I would gaze at myself, trying to decide what to wear, my room littered with rejected clothes. I felt fat and unattractive; nothing looked or felt right on me. Even my skin was tight and uncomfortable. Social situations, in which I increasingly felt no connection with people, made me feel concerned about how I was being judged. I thought I looked strange. I wondered how a forty-nine-year-old woman who had supposedly been mentally healthy all her life could suddenly feel so badly adjusted and unhealthy. Unhealthiness escalated and things became more extreme, making me feel as if I were crazy. I was operating in a time warp; time passed so slowly I felt out of sync. Leonard's death seemed both very recent and ages ago. I began mixing up dates. I wrote appointments on the wrong page in my date book so that one night I showed up at a friend's house for dinner and found no one at home. I was one week early!

The degree of my anxiety also made me feel crazy. It forced me to leave my house and rush into the city, only to discover I had no real reason to go to the city. Once, while riding on a crosstown bus, I saw a dark-haired man with a leonine head sitting several seats in front of me who looked so much like Leonard that my heart began to pound. Knowing full well that I was being irrational, I watched him get up to leave the bus. I got off too, to follow him, until he disappeared into an office building, leaving me shaken and frightened by my absurd behavior.

I did other weird things, more than once tossing out my bank statements without opening them, in the misguided belief that they were advertisements, and long after I had moved to the city, realizing I had left clothes at the old dry cleaners. What exactly was wrong with me? What did I have?

I was frightened enough to begin rereading my reference books. What were the diagnostic criteria for various mental illnesses? "Narcissistic Personality"? No. Then I looked up "Identity Disorder"—"Severe subjective distress regarding uncertainty, including (1) sexual orientations and behavior,

(2) long-term goals, (3) career choice, (4) religious identification, (5) moral value systems, (6) group loyalties, (7) friendship patterns." I had symptoms 2, 3, 5, and 7!

I looked up more diseases: "Anxiety Disorders," "Stress Disorders," "Hypochondrias," "Traumatic Neuroses"—I had some symptoms of almost *all* of them! Terrified that I was going to crack apart, I couldn't imagine how I was able to function professionally. I worried about it until it occurred to me that these symptoms only surfaced at home or among groups. They didn't appear when I was working. I was able to put them on hold while I shifted into other people's lives. First, I told myself, it was because I was operating from a technical base and my clinical skills were still in place. That explanation satisfied me until I realized it was more than that. My work was providing me with the mirroring I had lost; I was deeply involved with other people's issues, validating, reinforcing, and encouraging them. We were interacting, and I had stopped caring only about me.

You hardly need to be a therapist to find your way of establishing and redefining yourself. It may be, as it was with me, through your work, or through friendships, or people in your community who need you to help—anything that mirrors you.

Two years after Leonard died, a woman came to my office who had recently been widowed. She spoke in a wispy, little-girl voice about her friends, who were nonsupportive and increasingly unavailable. She still had a few people in her life whom she called friends, but felt she was doing what they wanted her to do, not what she cared about. Because of her talent with figures, they wanted her to return to school, get an MBA, and work on Wall Street. She was very clear about her feelings that she must live up to their expectations for her because she was so dependent on them in her time of crisis.

However, with no financial worries of her own, she wasn't the least bit interested in having a traditional job. Instinctively she felt she would flourish in a setting where her talent for giving and helping would be appreciated, rather than in a business school or the financial world, which felt barren to her. She had become increasingly interested in the problem of children born with AIDS. Volunteers were desperately needed in hospitals to work with these children. But when she told her friends, they were appalled—"Haven't you had enough misery . . . enough sickness . . . enough ugliness?" Verbally she agreed with them, but with each encounter she felt less herself and more helpless.

When she applied to several graduate schools, her friends applauded, not realizing she was hoping she wouldn't be accepted. When she was accepted she became utterly perplexed. It had been eight months since her husband died and yet she was still feeling the absence of his mirroring. Should she continue to hold on to her friends' expectations for her, or should she do what she knew she wanted to do? She began to cope with the anxiety caused by her need to make her own decisions, instead of fulfilling the expectations of others.

I told her I once had a friend who insisted I could never wear black. She claimed black drained all the color from my face and made me look like a walking ghost. I believed her because when she said it, I had lost Leonard, my mirror. I stopped wearing black even though all my life black had been my best color. She was so positive and so unbelievably assertive that I let her define me.

This was a trivial example, but it worked for my patient.

She immediately related to my experience. She said, "Screw your friend. People always think they know what's best for you, but they don't. You look great in black."

The fact is, it was my friend who couldn't wear black. My patient and I were victims of our friends' projections, and we were expected to meet some image they had of us. My patient vowed never to listen to people who were influencing her into doing things that made *them* feel good. She went to work in a children's ward, where she thrived. She was reoriented into a world in which her needs were being met. She had found a mirror.

Though I too had the vastly important reflection of self-worth that my work restored to me, I was still shaken by the loss of my mirror. I knew I had no choice but to look in other areas for other mirrors. Somehow I knew they had to be there and I would find them.

Can You Remember Before?

I remember looking at a photograph of Leonard taken the summer before he became ill. I was staring at it three weeks after he died, feeling as if I were looking at a movie star: someone I'd seen many times but had never met. It was a familiar picture but strangely at odds with the one in my head. The one I was looking at showed a healthy, vigorous, hearty man with thick gray hair, while the picture in my head was of a pale, bald, dying man. It was impossible to believe they were the same person.

My confusion about pictures was symptomatic of my confusion about all aspects of Leonard and of our marriage. I tried to recall our nineteen years and five months together before Leonard became ill, but no matter how hard I tried I couldn't. All I was able to see was the six-month period of hospitals, illness, and pain. Immediately following his death, my memories of our marriage before his illness were not accessible. It was as if we had had two marriages, two relationships. I was stuck in the immediate past, which felt like the present.

This past was grim: Leonard's illness first weakened our relationship and eventually destroyed it. He was preoccupied only with himself and his survival. We were living in two separate worlds; we had very little to say to each other since we had in fact nothing to share or bind us together. We were untied—disconnected. I would make an enormous effort to get to the hospital every day, often arriving exhausted and anxious. Leonard wasn't at all happy to see me. My entrances into his room felt, to me, like an invasion of his private world. He was interested only in his doctors— they could save him; I could not. If I was at odds with them in any way, he would be furious with me—they knew everything and I knew nothing.

His doctors treated me like a necessary evil—necessary for him, evil for them. Getting information was almost an impossibility. When I insisted on knowing something, they told it to me gracelessly and with reluctance. They could have been a bridge between the living and the dying, but chose not to be for their own emotional convenience.

A physician friend told me that he was taught in medical school how *not* to relate to the family of the terminally ill. There is a theory that doctors have a minimum of emotional energy that shouldn't be wasted on the family, but must be saved for the patient. It's a theory with some validity: doctors who deal with dying patients day after day quickly use up their supply of human warmth. Therefore the spouses usually receive cold, often harsh, treatment.

Leonard looked forward to his doctors' visits, not mine. We began to fight about them and other things—he resented the contrast between my vital and active existence and his isolated, impoverished, empty one. Our relationship shifted to a place in which I was the caretaker, he the patient. How he resented it! He demanded control over me as a way of dealing with his loss of control over everything else in his life. "Do" and "don't" became his favorite words. My volatile reaction followed. We argued about friends, money, children—all things about which we had never disagreed before. Where was the old us? I wondered. When I looked, we were gone forever. I blamed myself—I didn't treat him well, I wasn't tolerant.

Leonard became as difficult to deal with as an angry child. I couldn't handle all the things he wanted me to do. "Should" and "shouldn't" became *my* favorite words. I should have been kinder, nicer, better. I shouldn't have felt angry, abandoned, unwanted. I had to find a way to stop beating myself for my anguished emotions. I was not always the perfect wife for Leonard, sick or well, nor was he always the perfect husband. My guilt about my behavior and feelings during his illness pervaded my memories of my entire marriage. These feelings that I was incapable of perfect love, that I didn't value him enough, and that I had been moody obsessed me. I ruminated constantly about my mixed feelings. They made me so anxious I denied them, and the more I denied them the guiltier I felt. I went around in circles. I wanted so much to see Leonard as a perfect man, a perfect love, and part of a perfect relationship. But we had our negative qualities and we had our anger, and no matter how many circles I made around them, I finally had to acknowledge and accept their reality.

I began to see the real Leonard and the real me with all our flaws and imperfections—our good selves, our bad selves, and our mixed feelings about each other. Gradually I was able to see us from the beginning of our marriage to its end. And gradually the photograph in the picture frame and the one in my head came together. I know now from my own experience that one of the first pieces of business for widows is to stop idealizing and enshrining our partners. The longer we keep it up the longer we stay stuck with our guilt, our ambivalence, and our truncated existence.

But how do we stop? One of the techniques I learned to do with myself and that I used later with my widowed patients was to find ways of saying things that I wished I'd said when I'd had the chance.

Joanna, widowed fifteen months, came for therapy because she said she was unable to function either at home or at work. Her mind was totally focused on her failure to see that her husband was ill before his fatal heart attack. She was convinced she could have saved him if only she had seen the signs that she believed were there.

I encouraged her to talk about her marriage. She described it in glowing terms. It had been a beautiful union in which nothing ever went wrong—in which there were no fights and harmony was ever present. Her husband had been considerate, loving, and, to use her phrase, "the perfect person." She repeated this description many times until in the middle of her sixth session she interjected the fact that he had been an alcoholic. Her admission staggered her, but once having made it, she seemed somewhat relieved.

As we talked, a new note gradually crept into her associations and descriptions. She began to express resentment toward him for drinking. When he chose alcohol over being with her and her children, it always felt to her like desertion. But she was never able to *show* her anger. One day she blurted out to me, "Sometimes I almost hated him because he wouldn't stop." That was a revelation, but it was also scary to her. She went back to focusing on her failures and inadequacies. She had a major case of the "should-haves."

So many of her "should-haves" came from her inability to alter her present situation. The finality of her husband's death had closed off all opportunities for change. Years before, I had learned an effective therapeutic technique to deal with the dilemma of unfinished business. I suggested it would help her if she wrote a letter to her late husband, telling him *all* of her feelings about him, about them, about their marriage—and about her feelings of guilt. It sounded silly to her, but since I was the therapist, she reluctantly agreed to try. Her letter was incredible. She was able to start at the beginning of their marriage and piece by piece write about it, good parts and bad—her love and respect for him, his failures and her anger with him for them.

After she read me the letter, we talked about both her positive and negative feelings toward her husband. I suggested she answer the letter for her husband, since she knew him and his thinking so well. It took several weeks before she did it, but then she brought in a letter in which her husband acknowledged his excessive drinking, drinking that had cost him, to his deep regret, the loss of other major relationships in his life. He went on to say that he missed her and wished she would stop hitting herself in the head for not knowing he had been ill. "How could you have known?" he asked in the letter. "I didn't, the doctors didn't. What could have made you so omniscient?"

He teasingly recalled fights they had had, stressing his role in them and begging her to let go and get on with her life. He ended his letter by saying, "Kill the guilts before they kill you. I'll always love you." She cried through the entire session.

At the same time, she and I both knew she was on her way. She began to lose the feeling of guilty responsibility for her husband's death. Her mood and functioning capacity improved. She found renewed interest in people as well as in the activities that had formerly given her pleasure. She was able to stop focusing on her guilt and deal with other feelings. Now she could experience the pain of loss. Gradually she worked through her feelings of grief and emerged at the end of her treatment free of obsessing and free of guilt and with a renewed interest in living. Her mixed feelings toward her husband now coexisted peacefully: opposite sides of the same coin. She could stop thinking only about his death. Finally she could see him and their marriage in its entirety.

Not until Leonard had been dead eight months was I able to write my own letter and Leonard's response.

MY LETTER

Dear Leonard,

I miss you so much I don't even know where to begin. I had no idea it would be so hard because I thought somehow, by accepting the inevitability of your death, I could handle it without falling apart. After all, I had six months while you were hospitalized to prepare and practice being alone. What crap! I saw you at least once every day. In the morning you'd call to say hello and at night you'd call to say you loved me. You were, as always, the major part of my life. Now I'm not sure I can make it. I'm eaten up

alive by those last weeks in the hospital; I am obsessed by my failure to give you what you needed.
There weren't any hugs or even touching. What a
bitch I was! Fear, anger, and complete exhaustion
finally got the better of me. I was running from dawn
to midnight every day for months without much food
or sleep and my workload was staggering. I struggled through it all to get to the hospital, always dread-
ing the worst. Toward the end—oh, God, I can hardly
write the word—*hoping* for the *worst*. Isn't that awful?

Life felt intolerable, watching you struggle day after day with your pain, knowing you knew you were
dying. Enough, I said to myself, enough. But did I
mean enough for you, or enough for me? Maybe
both. How could I have been so disgusting? There
you were fighting to stay alive while I was saying
"Enough!" I couldn't deal with your slow disintegra-
tion. Hurry up, I whispered, if you're going to die do
it now. Little did I know that very, very soon I would
long for you just as you were: in the hospital, in that
metal bed, sick, dying, but still my life.

I wonder if you knew what I was thinking? I doubt
it since you had great difficulty seeing me in any way
except surrounded by golden lights. You even had
trouble remembering fights that I provoked out of my
neurotic need. I pushed and pulled until you finally
joined me in ugly, destructive arguments. God, what
a waste! Now I'll never have a chance to make it
better.

What should I do? I finally am in touch with my
miserable self. When I was little my mother told me
I was naughty and bad. What a riot—after all our
yelling she turns out to be right. Only an evil, unde-

serving, loathsome person could have my ugly, angry feelings.

Why am I writing to you now? I want you to know I'm not what I wanted to be. I failed you both during and at the end of our marriage. You were the cello talent of the century, worshiped by your audiences and your students. My respect and admiration for you had no limits but because of my difficulty with the demands that went with your talent, I often failed to show you how I really felt. Too often I was impatient and irreverent, instead of revering you as you deserved. I was Miss Know-it-all, the skillful analyst, Miss Verbal with all the answers. You deserved better.

I'll stop now, but I'll write soon again. I guess I'm looking for forgiveness, which my bad self knows I don't deserve.

> But—I love you,
> Xenia

LEONARD'S ANSWER

Dear Xenia,

I was both touched and saddened by your letter and don't know what to answer first. I guess the best way is to try to deal with it point by point. But first, take a deep breath and relax! Try, my love, to get off your own back a little so that you can read what I need to say to you.

You will never fall apart. As much as you're hurting, try to remember you're strong as an ox: competent and functional no matter what. How else could you have managed those six months all by yourself which, in case you don't know it, you did. Long hours at work and running back and forth to hospitals must have been a nightmare—you were living like a trapped animal.

You say you became angry, and why wouldn't you? I was angry-making! I had shut down and locked you out. I was too busy playing the well-adjusted, charming, reasonable dying man, getting admiration and applause. You know how much I loved applause, and I felt, oddly, that I had replaced my concert audience with the hospital staff. Dying well was my daily priority. I didn't want to, or couldn't (I'm not sure which), feel anything about dying itself. My robot act kept me protected. It also kept me sealed off from you and us.

If I had let myself feel, the pain of leaving everything—our beautiful home, our adorable cat, and above all my Xenia—would have been intolerable. Instead I felt nothing and gave nothing, which made you angry. It wasn't the first time. Those fights you mentioned were not all one-sided. We were two people who knew instinctively which buttons to push to get a reaction. I withdrew—I cut myself off from people and you fought to bring me back.

What a hell-raiser you are—a pot-stirrer, a real scrapper who forced me to deal with you. You were a people-person married to an obsessed musician who without you would have practiced eighteen hours a day. You helped me have a life with more—so much more in it—than playing the cello. Yes, my love, you can be a real pain in the ass. You know it and I do too, but you also know what's important and valuable. Those fights helped me connect to people, which I was never able to do before I married you. You helped me deal with my children after years of my pretending they didn't exist. You taught me to care about people and their problems. Most of all, you taught me to have fun—something I didn't have enough time to become really good at, but something I loved doing.

You are so hard on yourself when you talk about wishing I'd hurry up and die. My God, do you think you're the only person who has had those feelings? Your life was on hold for six months. It must have felt as if you were hanging on a hook waiting for what you knew from day one was inevitable. The physical drain coupled with your emotional turmoil would make anyone wish it were over—and, my love, you are an anyone! You *are* human. You had been through two long terminal illnesses with your parents; you must have felt you were getting a Ph.D. in death: hospitals, doctors, pain, endless waiting. Stop picking on you. You were a good, strong, responsible daughter and, if not a perfect wife, close to it.

As for your lack of reverence, I loved it. I've told you many times people who tend toward pomposity and grandiosity need and want a kick in the behind. You never tried to knock me off my pedestal: on the contrary, you joined me on it and together we sorted out the phonies and pretenders from the rest of our world.

I've reread your letter several times. You give yourself such a hard time. What was it you always called it? "A harsh super-ego." I'm not sure I know exactly what it means but it sounds right for you, constantly hitting yourself in the head for not meeting crazy and basically unmeetable demands. Stop, I beg you. Begin to let go of your constant self-criticism and self-doubts which have you stuck in the muck. Get out quickly. You're a woman with many years of living ahead. Get moving—I'll help you as much as I can.

Write me more if you need me,

And I love you too,

L.

Children: The First Important Man in Their Lives

As Leonard's condition worsened I had thought increasingly about our decision not to have children. At the very least a child or two could have offered needed support to Leonard and me through those harrowing months. And what about after? I would be alone—absolutely alone—with no major connection in my life.

Day after day, sitting in the hospital, I fantasized about a boy and girl we'd never had, picturing them growing into adults. They would have been with us now, loving, supporting, facilitating. They would have been my reason to keep going.

I kept those fantasies to myself, but after Leonard died I began a game of who's got it worse, me or widows with children? I talked with Claudia, a widowed friend with two teenage daughters. Suzie, thirteen, learned of her father's fatal car accident from her teacher. She immediately rushed home to take care of her mother. Suddenly the caretaker, Suzie was quiet, somber, and totally controlled. She notified relatives, helped with the funeral arrangements, and carefully dealt with her mother's increasing dependency.

Her sixteen-year-old sister Julie also learned of the accident from her teacher, but didn't come home until late that night. Confronting her mother, she turned on her in a rage, saying that she was leaving home to live with a friend whose "mother would have had the guts to tell her daughter herself instead of sending a messenger!" Julie's language, never too pure, was now punctuated with four-letter words at the end of every sentence. Life "sucked"; everything was "shitty" or "fucked-up." "I'll be goddamned if I need *you*!" Julia screamed at Claudia. Mad at the world, Julie had lost her beloved Daddy, whom she had worshiped from infancy.

At odds with her mother for years as she struggled through adolescence, Julie now let the war escalate sharply. She stayed away from home for most of the days preceding the funeral and afterward did move in with her friend. Previously on the dean's list, Julie now began failing major courses. She blamed her mother for her father's death, saying that Claudia had taken the better car the day of the accident. Her look changed as she altered her way of dressing, going from sophisticated sports outfits to childlike pinafores that made her look years younger.

Claudia wanted my advice, both as a friend and as a professional. As a therapist I was more concerned with Suzie than Julie. Suzie, solicitous and anxious about her mother, had become a thirteen-year-old adult, in charge and in control of running the home. As her mother went through mourning, Suzie showed no signs of loss or grief for her father, whom she too had adored. Claudia's view of Suzie as the "perfect child" was at variance with mine. Having lost her father, Suzie was now terrified of loss and was being "perfect" to protect herself from a second loss. If one parent can die, so can two. She was also struggling with her guilt concerning an argument she'd had with her father the night before his accident. He wanted her to practice the piano and she had refused. Now she was blaming herself for his death, convinced somehow that if she had done as he asked, he would still be alive. Fear, guilt, anger, denial— Suzie was hiding feelings very much like her mother's, but while she was allowing her mother to work through her feelings, she was not doing the same for herself.

Paradoxically, Julie was basically healthier, but she too was in trouble. She talked to me about her rage at everyone. She wanted most to be a little girl again, so that everything would be the way it had been, while now she felt everyone expected her to be an adult. But if she hadn't been one before her father died, how could she be one now?

Julie was deeply preoccupied with dying, saying she hadn't given it any thought before, but after her father's death she realized death could come to anyone, anytime— and she might be next. She also found herself becoming isolated by her father's death, having increasingly fewer friends: they had two parents, she had only one, so they and she no longer had anything in common.

As a professional I sympathized with Julie's wretchedness, but as a friend I sympathized with Claudia, whose life was in turmoil. She constantly worried about Julie, asking me, "Aren't you glad you don't have children?"

"Yes," I said, hesitantly, knowing what it was like to deal with Julie, but also wishing I had someone to worry over. I felt sure that Suzie and Julie would work out their problems, and no matter how long it took, the family would emerge connected to one another.

I felt much the same way about my patient Beverly, the mother of eight-year-old Keith. Only thirty, Beverly was mourning the death of her husband from a heart attack and dealing with the prospect of bringing up Keith by herself.

Her biggest problem was coping with his grief. Keith was severely depressed; he cried constantly, slept little, wet his bed, and often refused to go to school. He and his father had ritualistically played mini-pool before his bedtime and now Keith insisted on playing the game by himself. When Beverly intervened, Keith would sob hysterically and beg her to bring his father back.

Beverly felt helpless and trapped. She experienced Keith's misery as an impediment to overcoming her own grief and said, "The minute I begin to feel better, Keith screams for Daddy, which plunges me right back to the beginning. If he could shape up, I could too."

She became so frenzied by Keith that she decided to send him to his grandmother's for the summer. I interceded, cautioning her that Keith could easily feel he was losing two parents instead of one. He might also suffer from rejection and punishment by his mother, whom he needed now more than ever. Beverly took my advice, slowly beginning to deal with Keith's mourning as well as her own—healing herself as he healed. Within a year she could let Keith be unhappy without feeling his unhappiness for him, something she had been unable to do before. Now she was willing to let him sift through his feelings without intruding.

Widows like Claudia and Beverly have problems specific to young children, while widows with grown children have older versions of the same problems. Adult children faced with the death of their fathers often become dependent, frightened, and lost as their family of origin slips away. Daddy or Papa, the first serious, competent, attractive man in their lives, is gone. The small-child part of our adult children screams, "Daddy, come back, I need you!" They are left with us, their mothers.

Sybil's daughter could barely conceal her disappointment

that it was her father who had died instead of her mother, whom she thought of as "the burden." She then felt so guilty she phoned her mother every day from the West Coast to make sure she was okay. Another widow's son couldn't decide how dependent on him he could allow his mother to be. He was critical of her repeated requests for advice, but was angry when she made decisions on her own. He punished her coming and going.

Dependence versus independence: your struggle and theirs. Life is different from what it's ever been; all the old rules and expectations have been changed. How much of them do you need and what do they need from you? How much do they need you to need them? It's a tangle—and, conceivably, a disaster.

A young patient asked, "Can I still go away to college now that Dad is dead? What if Mom can't make it alone?"

His mother was sending mixed messages, wanting him to stay but knowing it would be healthier for him to go. They found their way out of the mix-up by talking about it, his mother finally deciding to return to college herself to get her degree. Now my young patient was forced to deal with *his* feelings of being away, alone, and with the beginnings of his adulthood.

Death changes all relationships, and the more important the relationship the more vast the changes. I've worked with forty-year-olds with families of their own for whom the loss of a father was a devastating blow. Unresolved issues, unfinished business with their first loved male person, can and often does turn their lives inside out. Husbands, children, friends, and siblings can get caught in the chaos that follows death. Changes in living, inheritances, and failed expectations often provide long-delayed confrontations.

My stepchildren dealt with their father's death in different ways. Leonard's daughter, my friend for life, continues her battle to overcome remaining obstacles. His son, however, went a different route. He disappeared in a cloud of rage. Historically he deeply resented his father's limited talent for parenting. Now he displaces his feeling onto me, finding relief only by severing all connections with me and with his sister. Perhaps someday he will return to renegotiate and reinstate both relationships. Perhaps.

Like so many adults, my stepson failed to make the transition from primary to secondary family—he continues to focus the bulk of his energies on Leonard, his sister, and me, instead of on his wife and young son. The "what-ifs" and "should-have-beens" took precedence over the "what's-going-on-now."

My stepson's reaction made me recall Wendy, a patient referred to me after her father died. She had devoted all her time to him during the nine months of his illness, leaving her fourteen-year-old daughter, Joan, and her husband, Randel, to care for each other.

She returned home from the funeral saying, "Dad is dead, I have nothing to live for." All of her previous responsibilities at home were now beyond her. She withdrew into a shell of depression as her mourning deepened. Her husband and daughter tried a number of tactics in attempts to connect with her, desperately trying to pull her out of her shell and back to them. But all support, confrontations, and accusations failed. Joan began acting out at school, cutting classes and fighting with her friends. A teacher, seeing Joan's distress, called her mother. Wendy was able to grasp the situation and heed the advice to see me. She told me that when she was four her mother had died, leaving her and her father alone. He christened her "woman of the house," which she loved, until at thirteen she was faced with her father's remarriage to a widow with three children. Devastated and displaced, Wendy was lost in her new world. She fantasized about plane crashes that would leave her an orphan and dreamed about holdups in which her father was killed.

On her twenty-first birthday Wendy married a young doctor, Randel, finding a solid, happy, contented life with him and then with their little girl, until unfinished business with her father changed everything. Her guilt over her anger during adolescence, her unresolved feelings of loss for her mother, her rage fantasies—all suppressed till now—surfaced. Those feelings, locked away for sixteen years, needed to be acknowledged, explored, felt once again, and finally resolved. Only at that point could Wendy reconnect with her husband and daughter.

Children of all ages who have lost their fathers go through a different version of adult mourning. There are many stages—numbness, shock, anger, denial, disorientation, depression, guilt, panic, and acceptance (not necessarily in that order), all similar to adult mourning. But children say it their way—"help me" . . . "protect me" . . . "don't make me feel too needy" . . . "let me grow up" . . . "let me not grow up" . . . "I'm okay" . . . "I'm not okay."

We share the same loss. The one person in the whole world who could have made it better is gone forever. Your children are traveling through their new world much the same way as you are. They need love and understanding, and to be in surroundings where they are free to express their feelings. Your children will find their way as you find yours.

Patterns of Competition

I was trying to give up the guilts and get going, when I felt myself under siege from my favorite child, Leonard's grown daughter. She and I had at last developed a close relationship, and during his illness she was loving and unshakable. We strengthened and supported each other through the worst days, and after Leonard's death we became even closer. However, now when Leonard was being honored by various musical groups and organizations, it suddenly felt as if there were two widows instead of one widow and one lost, adult child.

As Leonard's widow I felt forced to defend my province. Everywhere I was invited, his daughter insisted on being included. And worse—if I didn't go, she went in my place, finally getting the part she had always longed for. It felt as if we were locked in combat—she wanted more of Leonard than I cared to give up: an old and unresolved issue. One day she told me how she had gone to a memorial concert where she had been treated exactly like her mother, Leonard's first wife. "Now it's my turn," she said. She was locked in two fights—one with her real mother and one with me.

We talked for hours and hours on the telephone and over coffee. It was frightening because we were saying things we'd never been able to say before. She felt ugly and competitive about her relationship with me for her father. Already knowing about this situation from Leonard, I was able to tell her how differently I felt and how much Leonard had cared about her. Yes, I had my own competitive position to protect; I wanted to be remembered as the center of Leonard's world, but I discovered that the center had room for both his daughter and for me. Carefully she and I redefined ourselves in relation to each other and to Leonard. The competition stopped.

Unfortunately she was only one of many competitors—others complained that they were in the greatest pain over Leonard's loss. Friends were high up on the list. I had one who stopped calling almost immediately after the funeral. We had been so close we almost breathed together. She and her husband and Leonard and I had relished our social life. We were joined by shared interests and common metabolisms—he a passionate surgeon and she a child psychologist. We seemed connected on all sides: men to men, women to women, and women to men. How unusual and how special we thought we were. She was particularly active in pursuing the relationship, treasuring our foursome as much as we did.

But after the funeral she vanished, taking her husband with her. She didn't call, nor did she return my calls. I was shocked, hurt, and completely astonished. I wrote her a long, confrontational, questioning letter. Her response came quickly by telephone. She said that looking at me made her and her husband think about Leonard, which they did not want to do. They were moving along briskly with their lives and any reminder of Leonard would slow them down. Clearly a transaction with me would cause instant pain, which they chose not to suffer. She went on to suggest that her hurt was far greater than mine, presenting me with her analyst's theory of Leonard's being a father figure for her as well as a friend—so of course she was having more trouble than I was: I had only lost a husband, whereas she had lost both a father and a friend.

Other competitions continued. An elderly relative, widowed two months after I was, challenged me at dinner one night, claiming her loss was more important than mine because her husband didn't travel, suggesting that absence signified a less meaningful relationship. She deserved more pity, she thought, because her marriage had been better (after all, her husband stayed home), overlooking the fact that she was eighty and I was forty-nine.

Anyone can play the game. A colorful example is Betty, a patient, whose adult daughter Lena had been her father's most pampered possession. Betty was very angry during her first session—angry at her newly deceased husband, her friends, her sister, her other two children. But not at her princess Lena. Betty clearly felt inadequate to handle all the problems her husband's death had caused, explaining that he had always taken care of everything, leaving her as helpless as a child. Even at the first session she described herself as a shadowy figure in the family system that had focused on Lena, a flawless beauty with a talent for both the flute and the piano.

Betty's husband, a lawyer, had amassed a small fortune by the time he died of an embolism at the age of fifty-nine. During his life Betty's role in the family was to be a dutiful, perfect wife and mother to her two boys while her husband, Doug, took full responsibility for Lena's upbringing.

As my patient presented Lena, she sounded both awed and impressed by her, but at the same time she let me see Lena as a supercontrolling, overpowering, overbearing young woman, very much like her father. Betty was in a rage at the world without being able to identify its major cause. She had covertly dealt with Lena, her competitor since birth, but now the covert was overt. She tried to understand her mixed feelings but she was still too stuck with her husband's idealized image of Lena to see the Bad Seed's intrusion in her present life.

Lena dominated all the postfuneral social interactions,

making sure people always asked. "How's poor Lena? Is she all right?" and "What a painful melancholia—when will it be over so she can play her flute again?" Lena had strict expectations for her mother during the mourning period, including taking care of her two babies so that she could remain immobilized with grief. Grandmother would become mother once again while she, Lena, became the grieving widow. Could anyone afford to care about her mother, my patient?

This situation continued for several months. Betty and I talked but nothing changed until one day I suggested we role-play, letting me take Lena's part. It shifted our work into a more useful and pragmatic place. We role-played further, with my becoming increasingly narcissistic and bitchy, until at one session I said, as Lena to her mother, "You're a weak, insignificant, silly woman whom Daddy barely tolerated . . . he loved me best in the whole world, not you!"

Betty, finally ready, yelled at me, "You're a goddamn brat! You're spoiled and nasty. How do you think it was for me all those years playing second fiddle!" And she began to laugh!

We stopped role-playing long enough to deal with her very mixed feelings about Lena and Doug. When we picked up role-playing again, Betty said, "Listen, let's get one thing straight, I'm the widow, not you!" Good things were on the way for both Lena and her mother.

Competition, power, strength, and weakness in a family—all are set in place before tragedy strikes. We tend to forget how our family system worked. Your family's patterns of dealing with one another before loss very likely set the scene for what occurs afterward.

Della, another example of past patterns of behavior

played out after death, originally felt strongly that her daughter's destructive behavior was a result of her father's death from a brain tumor. Sally, the teenage daughter, had erupted into full-fledged rebellion against her mother by staying out past curfew and talking about experimenting with drugs.

Della couldn't talk about her daughter in any detail prior to her husband's death. However, she was able, in elaborate detail, to describe Sally and her relationship with her during the ordeal as both supportive and loving. I tried to get Della to think about Sally when she was very young. What had she been like? What roles did the family take? How did Sally fit into my patient's relationship with her husband?

It didn't take long before Della shyly asked what it meant that Sally was now blaming her for her husband's death. Sally's position was that she, Sally, loved her father more than her mother had, and if *she* had been in charge, *her* love would have saved him. It felt like competition to my patient, as indeed it was. After some exploration it became clear that Sally and her mother had never resolved their lifetime competitive feelings. I asked to see Sally and her mother jointly to talk about these issues. Both willingly agreed.

Della was able to tell her daughter she was tired of having her friends more interested in Sally's problems and reactions than in her own. Sally seemed surprised that her mother's friends were so concerned about her, but then admitted she was glad she was finally the center attraction that she'd always wanted to be. Mother and daughter argued loudly with each other, opening up chronic angers and resentments. Weeks later they began to resolve their conflicts and to see that they were victims of a death that blew the lid off their hidden rivalries for a husband and a father.

These examples may not be similar to your experience so far, but sooner or later you are likely to find yourself competing to express your grief. A friend told me that every time she saw her mother-in-law, she found herself taking a backseat as the woman listed her agonies over losing a son. "The worst loss anyone can suffer is the loss of one's child," she repeatedly asserted. My friend, the widow, didn't dare talk about how she felt.

You have to find a way to express your grief no matter how difficult it can seem. Perhaps you are grappling with questions about how often you can show your feelings to your children. You're probably protecting them, assuming that seeing you in tears would upset them more than they already are. However, if you don't allow yourself to cry, you may worry that they'll think you don't care, that you didn't love Dad.

It's a double bind—you're doomed if you grieve aloud and doomed if you don't. Perhaps you decide to share a recollection of a happy intimacy you had with their father— only to have them tell you in turn that they experienced it quite differently. They look back on the same incident feeling envious, excluded, and resentful. It seems like the movie *Rashomon*—memories from totally different perspectives.

Whatever you're doing, it probably feels wrong. You have so many questions, too much to do, and above all, find yourself competing with a lot of people for attention and reinforcement. Tell yourself to take one step, one day, one problem at a time. The time will come when you'll know that the competition had more to do with the competitors than it had to do with you.

4

Turning Points

Revelations

One Sunday, late in the afternoon, having done as much packing for my upcoming move as I could endure, I found myself at loose ends. I telephoned a few friends but none were at home so I decided to go to a movie. I had been to very few since Leonard died because my choices were limited: movies couldn't be about illness, death, or related subjects. Now I checked the movie guide and decided to see *Amadeus*— a remarkable choice since music was one of those related subjects. I hadn't been able to listen to any music after Leonard's funeral, which was filled with music. No records, no radio, and, except for one concert played by Leonard's most remarkable student, Yo-Yo Ma, I hadn't been to any concerts.

Yo-Yo played one night, shortly after Leonard died, with the New York Philharmonic and asked me to be his guest. Yo-Yo and I have a very special relationship based on twenty-five years of closeness. He is my "I-wish-I-could-have-adopted" son, whom Leonard and I parented through many chaotic growing periods, and for whom Leonard or I would have walked through fire if Yo-Yo had required it. Leonard's death had brought us even closer than before—Yo-Yo lost not only a revered teacher, but an all-encompassing father figure as well. He and I clung to each other in the months following Leonard's death—he taking care of his widowed "mother," I intensely aware of his double loss. We were in constant touch, and when he invited me to his solo appearance with the New York Philharmonic, I accepted with very little regard for the consequences.

It was a disaster. The minute I entered Avery Fisher Hall I knew I had made a major error. It was all painfully familiar: the usual audience surrounding me, the members of the orchestra in their seats warming up, and in the center of the stage the soloist's chair, raised on a podium, waiting, empty. I had seen a chair like this one in this hall for twenty years, waiting for Leonard. Now the chair was waiting for Yo-Yo.

Looking at the chair brought back memories of another death, another loss, over twenty years before, when John F. Kennedy was assassinated. I had wept for days and now I remembered his funeral cortege, led by a riderless horse—the empty saddle with its stirrups reversed, symbolizing the loss of our Commander-in-Chief. Leonard's chair was that horse—a symbol of emptiness and abandonment.

I stayed rooted to my seat in the concert hall, and minutes later Yo-Yo walked from the wings to be greeted by enthusiastic applause. He played tormentingly familiar music, looking handsome and securely adult. The mantle had discernibly been passed.

By the end of the concert I was inconsolable; leaving the

hall I felt paralyzed. When I reached home I began to scream, vowing never to attend another cello concert or any other concert as long as I lived. Music would no longer be a part of my life. It couldn't give me its former pleasure, only pain. It belonged to the next generation of artists and their wives. I went so far as to give away many of my tapes and records. No more music in my life! Leonard's haunting cello sound had been silenced.

But music pursued me. I'd walk into shops where radios were playing classical music and leave quickly, without buying anything. Radios playing in taxicabs were volcanoes about to explode, and elevators with classical music were cages from which I couldn't escape. Music had once been a low hum in the background; now it became a shrieking focus. Don't listen, don't hear, don't respond, and you'll be fine, I sternly instructed myself.

Now six months had gone by and this Sunday afternoon I chose a movie about Mozart, knowing music would be its central theme. The play on which it was based had not included Mozart's music, but rather focused on his character, his life, his relationship with the musical community, his flight into insanity. I remembered the play as being a character study of the two principals, so I went despite the musical association.

When the lights went out, before the movie began, the theater was suddenly filled with glorious sounds coming from its loudspeakers. Mozart's Requiem—a hymn to death—reverberated through every pore of my body; I felt suspended in space, attached to nothing, elevated above the theater. I pictured an airplane way above the earth, bouncing in and out of clouds. Then the movie started, resounding with music—early, middle, and mature Mozart, each phase deepeningly incandescent. I was transformed by its glories. I felt as if I were ten pounds lighter, just sitting there. As the music soared, my spirit lightened as my burden began to lift. Music, music, Leonard's music, music through the ages, more effective than anything in books, more connected than voices or words. It released the dead parts of me that had always loved it before my marriage, as well as the part of me that worshiped Leonard's musical being—his passion, his relentless integrity, his unique talent, and his total commitment. Because I had loved this part of him so much, I had fled from the intolerable pain its loss had caused. Now I realized that what music had meant to him could in modified and very different ways mean the same to me. I didn't have to run away anymore because the pain was gone—I could love music now more than before, I could integrate it into my life, and by doing so keep Leonard a part of me always.

Judith Viorst, in *Necessary Losses*, talks about this whole process of integrating parts of people: "Remember that as children, we could let our mothers go, or leave our mothers by establishing a permanent mother within us. In a similar way we internalize, we take into ourselves the people we have loved and lost to death." Viorst quotes psychoanalyst Karl Abraham, who writes: "The love object is not gone, for now I carry it within myself." Again, Viorst says, "The touch is gone, the laugh is gone, the promise and possibilities are gone, the sharing of music and bread and bed is gone, the comforting, joy-giving, flesh-and-blood presence is gone—it is true nonetheless that by making the dead part of our inner world we will in some important ways never lose them. It is through identification that we can develop and enrich our emerging self."

My internalization of and identification with Leonard had a colossal impact. For the first time since his death I felt incredibly sad for *him*, instead of for me. Until I walked out of the movie, I had not been in touch with my heartbreak at what Leonard had lost when he died. I stood in the street outside the theater filled with emotions. Inspired by the film, my awareness of a major turning point, my joy at feeling the music with such intensity—all seemed intertwined with my new revelation of what Leonard had lost. He would not have the experience of the movie I had just seen or similar magical theatrical events. He would never again enjoy things he'd loved when he was alive—his trips, his work, his house, his hearty appreciation of a good meal and sexy sex, his adoration of our cat and of me. No longer would he smile when the first crocus poked its head through the ground after a long winter, and no longer would he delight in the changes of the seasons. All this time I had mourned the loss of Leonard only in relation to me, forgetting what had been lost for him. He would never have a chance to change further, to grow and explore. It saddened me to think of all the things death had deprived him of experiencing. And yet I knew that two turning points, one after the other, had happened and pushed me farther along.

There's only one *Amadeus* and my reaction was very personal. But other plays, movies, books—anything that takes you outside yourself and involves you in a new emotional experience—can serve as a turning point. Often such a moment comes without announcing itself or letting you know that's what it is. It can take months before you realize it's come and gone, and by that time you're probably in the middle of a new one.

Could You Use a Persian?

Another turning point presented itself at a time when I wasn't interested in anyone or anything and was feeling alone and isolated. I, of all people, could recognize the symptoms. I was depressed. "So what?" I asked myself. "Who cares?" My most overwhelming feeling was that I was in limbo, attached to nothing. John Clare's poem kept running through my head:

> A night without morning
> A trouble without end,
> A life of bitter scorning
> A world without a friend.

My world was without a friend or a major connection. I was appalled by the thought that if I left in the morning to go to work and didn't come home at night, no one would know or care. What if I was in an accident? I'd walk down the street staring at people, wondering who would go looking for them if they didn't show up at night. Who would care? I envied my widowed friend with children. She was still connected to people in a way that I was not. She was attached to and responsible for living things, her children, while I was attached to the dead—responsible to no one.

One of my friends tapped into this particular piece of my depression and suggested I get another pet. I said no emphatically. It would be a major demand that I couldn't meet. She tried reasoning with me, pointing out that I'd always had a cat when I was married, and even before that, as a child. She was right . . . but no thanks. The cat Leonard and I had had since its kittenhood was Pamplemousse, a calico alley cat who grew to be very much Leonard's pet. During

Leonard's illness, Pamplemousse changed, becoming more withdrawn and neurotic as she saw less and less of her adored and adoring master, who was able then to come home only on occasional weekends.

The day Leonard died, I came home alone as usual—and Pamplemousse headed straight for Leonard's closet and stayed in there, letting out blood-curdling cat screams. By the time I was ready to leave our suburban home weeks later and move into a Manhattan apartment, Pamplemousse represented a real problem: now sixteen, she had always been an indoor-outdoor cat and the vet told me it would constitute cruelty to move her into the city. I certainly didn't want to have her put down—it would have felt like a double wipe-out.

The postman came one morning and found me in front of the house crying over my plight. "Let me handle this," he said—and he did. He knew a woman cellist somewhere in town who had seventeen cats already—and the idea of adding Leonard Rose's pet to the group was a special thrill. Pamplemousse had found a home where she was treated as a star. Now I wanted to be free to go away weekends, and a pet would be an unnecessary burden. Perhaps later, I told my friend, but not now. She decided reason was not the best approach. She invited me to her country house for the weekend and while I was there she drove me to a cat breeder who just happened to have several litters of my favorite cats—Persian Himalayans. They were adorable: different colors, different personalities. Any one of them would have melted a normal heart. If I'd been me, I would have been thrilled with all of them—the brown one with blue eyes; the white one with emerald eyes—all tumbling on top of one another, fighting for a string or hitting a tiny white ball. I felt nothing, because I wasn't me. I had lost part of myself.

I was different and less than the person I used to be. I wasn't ready or able to love anyone or anything, not even a kitten. Let's go, I said, and we left.

Months went by. Periodically I would visualize one of the kittens I'd seen, but quickly put it out of my mind. A kitten would wreck my perfect, pristine apartment. Cats throw up. God forbid, they pee on expensive new carpets. I thought of litter boxes and their smell before you change them. In other words, I used every argument for not having a pet, because a pet represented the potential for even more loss. The thought was intolerable. I felt both restricted and constricted. Leonard's death was forcing me to find substitutes to meet my basic need to love and be loved, and yet my reaction to my loss was causing an emotional shutdown. Don't care about anyone or anything, I told myself. If you do, you're going to get hurt again.

Two forces were pulling me apart. One said don't care, don't connect, don't put yourself in a vulnerable place. On the other hand there was a part of me that wanted to care, wanted to connect and be in that place. My awareness of these conflicting and paradoxical feelings was in itself a turning point for me.

One of my patients sensed a turning point for her when she began to read the travel section of *The New York Times*. She was talking about the places she wanted to go to and thinking about air fares, hotel costs, and with whom she could travel. Suddenly she developed a host of painful somatic sensations. She felt tightness in her throat and shortness of breath. She came to her session complaining about her lack of strength and feelings of exhaustion, saying she could barely climb up a flight of stairs. She also complained of trouble eating. "Food tastes like sand and I have no appetite at all. My middle feels hollow. Everything has slowed down in my stomach." I pointed out that her symptoms reminded me of her early traumatic reactions to her husband's death. What was happening now to cause their return?

We explored her feelings, both her current ones and those she'd had after her husband died. She was able to talk about her fear of moving on, very much the same way she had talked about being alone and having to deal with all the issues and feelings that went with it. Perhaps it could mean giving up her newly discovered ways of coping.

Now she was sitting alone in her apartment after work, not liking it, but feeling competent and functioning. She had put together a life. Somehow the idea of going on a trip felt like getting back into the world: a turning point! Was it possible she would find her new coping skills didn't work? She was experiencing painful, panicky stress caused by the possibility of change.

Only after intense exploration and reinforcement of her new coping skills was she able to feel that her turning point was not a threat but a beginning. Her physical symptoms slowly dissipated, as did her anxiety about travel. The first postcard she sent me was from Istanbul.

A year after my friend had prematurely taken me to see the litters, I started going past pet shops and staring in the windows—at kittens, and always the same kind, Persian Himalayans. I began comparing fur colors, checking liveliness, and asking prices. Slowly I was moving, getting ready. And finally I *was* ready to begin an intensive search for my kitten. I discovered a computer bank in New Jersey that records births of different breeds of cats. They inform you as to when, where, and what cats are having litters and give you the names of the breeders to call. I was told of four litters of Persian Himalayans that were expected the following month. But all were due in Brooklyn, a place with which I had no familiarity. They laughed when I pleaded for a breeder in Westchester County. "You go where the kittens are, and right now that's Brooklyn."

I called two friends who had remained a part of my life. They knew the importance of my request for their aid in buying a kitten. One, a cat-hater, had grown up in Brooklyn and could get me through its maze of streets. The other, a cat-lover, knew her knowledge about cats and her support of me were a necessity.

We made appointments to see three breeders. My heart was set on a pure white kitten with green eyes. The first breeder we contacted sagely suggested I not make up my mind in advance, saying, "Kittens and people have a very special relationship. You won't know until you see the one you want—it's a love relationship."

What a day! We looked at twenty kittens. The breeder, of course, was right. I fell for a kitten with brown fur and yellow eyes. "Ugh," said my friend the cat-hater, "she's ugly!" But to me she was a beauty. The white ones with green eyes were cute, but not for me. The brown one was mine and I knew it the moment we saw each other. It was a match. I put down a deposit knowing I would have to be patient two months until she was old enough to leave her birth mother. In the meantime I would get ready: buying food, toys, a playhouse. I would soon become her new mother and couldn't wait. On the trip home from Brooklyn my friends and I felt exhilarated. Even the cat-hater realized something major had taken place. I was bubbling with excitement—I would soon have something to care for, something to love. I would be connected once again to a living thing.

When she finally came, that day I had so looked forward

to was a disaster. My yellow-eyed kitten, who looked so much like an owl that Owl became her name, spent the entire weekend under my bed. She was frightened by every new sound or movement. She didn't eat, play, or do anything kittenlike.

But slowly over the next few weeks she became my friend. First she played with her toys, and then with me. As we became closer she seemed almost human. One night when I was crying for Leonard, she leaped up on my bed. She put one paw on my face and looked intensely into my eyes. Don't do that anymore, she seemed to say, it's okay, I'm here for you.

Not everyone wants or needs a pet, but I have known many widows who have profited as much as I have from such a loving relationship.

Nora, who hadn't had a pet since she was nine, was sadly closing her summer home for the last time; the house was up for sale and she was moving back, alone, to a city apartment. Her husband had died four months ago and her grown children lived away from home. As she was struggling with the storm windows an unknown young man appeared with a shivering mongrel puppy in his arms. He'd found the little creature in the street and had checked every house but Nora's without finding the owner. What should he do now? The puppy looked straight into Nora's soul and won it.

"Wasn't I crazy?" she asked me a few days later, introducing me to Freebee cradled in her arms. Crazy, no. Nora, who had never exercised in her life, now walks for miles enjoying the park and Freebee, and Freebee is the reason she's considering buying another, smaller country house for the two of them.

Turning points can be anything—cats, dogs, birds, travel,

art, music, or work—and will be different for different individuals, but what they all have in common is growth and
change. You will know you've reached your turning point
when you feel the parts of you opening that were closed by
pain.

A Group for the Widowed

I was feeling better—and then I wasn't. I swung from one
mood to another; sometimes up, sometimes down. In one
frame of mind I told myself, "Life is going to get better." But
then my mind changed to, "I'm stuck, nothing will get
better."

The turning points had felt miraculous, but the miracles
didn't last. Depression had me in pain much of the time,
less acutely than in the beginning but nonetheless clawing
at me and refusing to let go.

On an intellectual level I understood that the mourning
process always includes extreme mood swings. On an emotional level, however, I was increasingly uneasy about my
frequent bouts with depression and fear that they would
never go away.

When *New York* magazine ran a lead story called "Depression," I looked at the woman's fragmented face on the cover
and immediately identified with it, a face with its spirit
shattered—a mosaic come unglued and lying in a chaotic
pile.

I studied the article on depression and its causes: What
component is physical? How much is psychological? What
can be treated and what cannot? All my symptoms were
described and validated. But despite a long list of sugges-

tions from experts in the field, there was nothing that felt like a prescription for me. I reread the piece with increasing panic that my depression would last forever. As I was about to toss the article aside as useless, I noticed a list of resources at the bottom of the last page. Widows and widowers were invited to join a trial group therapy session. The date, time, place, and a phone number for additional information were included. Immediately my defenses, supported by thirty years of elitism, swung into action. "I'm no joiner," I told myself. If groups are not psychoanalytic they are for alcoholics, fat people, dropouts, and lost souls. They're certainly not for smart, sophisticated people like me. Why would I want to listen to other people's miserable sobbing and sniveling? More important, I'm a therapist, not a patient! I was unable for the moment to remember that therapists who do their work well have been patients at one time or another. Our strongest skill is the resolution of our own problems; work done on ourselves is often used to help our patients.

I've talked with many widows since that dark afternoon, most of whom had similar emotions about entering a group. Joining seemed to represent the loss of uniqueness, a giving up of your own special experience for other people's histories. How could they possibly impinge helpfully on your own life? The thought of linking up with others can make you feel as if your specialness, although lonely and terrifying, is all there is. These are your tightly wrapped defenses that you hope will protect you from the overwhelming feelings of loss. Like so many defenses they worked in a healthy and positive way when you needed them most—during the period right after your husband died. They kept you intact and functioning. Now they may be working against you, serving to isolate you further. Joining a group is only one way to begin to let go of these defenses. Grief has to be shared if there is to be hope. Joining a group is a beginning.

I hated the idea of being needy enough to seek out a group. I hated being scared. I guess I hated me the most. And yet, after having hung up twice without completing my call, I finally left my telephone number with the group leader. I felt as if, despite my enormous resistance, I was at least and at last taking some action.

Two weeks later I went to the first meeting. It was hot and my anxiety was as high as the humidity. I was as usual a half hour early getting to the address and wandered around the neighborhood until the time finally arrived to go upstairs to the meeting room. Pat, the group leader, was waiting by the door. She led me in and introduced me to four women already seated. We looked at one another—all anxious and uncomfortable. More people arrived. Now there were eight of us, including two widowers. We ranged in age from the early twenties to the mid-sixties, and our clothes and overall appearances were equally diverse. There was only one thing we had in common: none of us wanted to be there.

Pat began by telling us briefly about herself. A social worker, she had been widowed nine years before when her husband died of a heart attack, leaving her with his two teenagers from a previous marriage. Pat raised them, and in the process of learning how to survive became convinced that she and widows like her needed a place to share their experience and feelings.

None of us looked at one another as she spoke. Instead we stared intently at her. It was as if she alone could help eight small children focused on one parent. She then suggested we go around the room talking a little bit about ourselves and our experiences.

Our "stories," as we came to call them, were as varied as
we were. Age, type of illness, cause and length of illness—
all were different circumstances. Two husbands had died of
cancer, one very swiftly, the other after an interminable two
years. There were two suicides, a heart attack, a stroke, one
death from kidney disease and one from diabetes. The people in the group had been widowed from just over a year,
like me, to eight years before. Some were articulate, others
barely spoke. When my turn came I had no sooner begun to
talk about Leonard than I broke into tears. I was astonished.
Was I still so raw after more than a year? I felt completely
out of control. But since almost everyone else was crying it
didn't seem to matter. Pat tactfully moved on to the next
person, who refused to talk at all. The silence felt chaotic.
There is something anxiety-provoking about being asked to
speak when you can't. I felt the silence would go on forever
until Betsy, seated on my left, began to talk. A middle-aged
researcher for a magazine, she had been married for twenty
years to a successful lawyer who had leaped from a boat and
drowned. He left a note blaming his business partner, with
whom he hadn't been able to get along, and financial re-
verses. Betsy spoke in disjointed sentences with a flat, inappropriate affect, her tone seeming to deny the reality of
what she was relating: she might as well have been talking
about what someone else had said happened. She seemed
somewhat isolated—she had no children, few friends, and
said she was joining the group for one simple reason: she
couldn't cry. She explained that she hadn't cried since "it"
happened.

The group greeted her story with silence. Then Norman,
heavyset and sweating, began to talk. A health-insurance
worker in his mid-forties, he was angry, very angry. His
face reddening as he spoke, he told of his wife's "inevita-

ble" stroke. Obese, she had smoked three packs of cigarettes a day, even though she'd been warned about her increasing bad health. But she had been unwilling or unable to change. Norman talked primarily about his profound feeling of isolation, which, it turned out, was a result of his inability to telephone or contact friends. His wife had managed all aspects of their social life and he now felt helpless. He couldn't do it for himself.

Beautiful Vera, only twenty-three, had jointly owned and operated a small restaurant, the stress of which she blamed for her young husband's heart attack. Now busier and more frantic than ever, trying to keep the café in business by herself, she was being terrified by midnight anxiety attacks. She would awaken with her heart thumping, sweating profusely and shaking from head to toe. She was convinced she was having a heart attack, as her husband had had before.

I knew *exactly* how she felt. After Leonard died, I was certain I had leukemia. I had every familiar symptom: the sores that didn't heal quickly, extreme fatigue, and leg cramps. I clung to these symptoms to stay close: he had them, I had them—we were still connected. This thinking is very common among survivors. It's a dance our subconscious does to maintain that connection with our lost partners.

Two somewhat older women refused to talk. They said they couldn't and we skipped over them.

Tall and balding Cliff, another widower, spoke softly and hesitantly of his concern for his eighteen-year-old daughter. He said they spent every evening and most weekends together. They had done this for the six months following his wife's death. Nothing had changed. He felt they were trapped.

Gray-haired Sybil, sixty-three years old and widowed four

months, couldn't tolerate being in her apartment. She'd be at home and '"have to get out." She'd seen almost every play and movie in New York. When she wasn't in a theater, she was shopping, buying clothes that she confessed she'd never wear.

By this time an hour had passed and Pat asked who would be returning next week for the second meeting. Six of us, not counting the two silent older women, agreed to come. Something unexpected had happened. We had begun to make sense out of the senseless. Despite all the differences, the bond of empathy and mutuality had become the foundation for our eventual climb out of the quicksand of despair. For me there was no choice. I had to come back because I had instantaneously felt the group's unconditional acceptance of my continuing unhappiness. Pat and the people in the group had created a safe surrounding in which I knew I could be me—a place where I wouldn't have to worry about how I was expected to behave or feel, a place where I could stop being concerned about how I was affecting other people. We were all separated from our past lives and needed the support the group could offer in our present lives.

We also needed to get to know one another. After all, we were strangers who under other circumstances would probably not be friends. But related by death we would learn to share our most intimate and embarrassed selves.

Week after week I struggled with issues, both mine and theirs. Vera needed help dealing with her husband's closet, which haunted her. Everyone in the group reacted. I immediately identified with her pain caused by the thought of giving away her late husband's clothes. I had left Leonard's closet exactly the way he had always kept it, the way it always looked when he was on tour: neat, well-organized, and ready for immediate decisions. It made me feel as if he could return at any moment. Also, even after many months, his clothes still had Leonard's scent. Emptying his closet seemed like an impossible task. And yet I finally let go.

There are different ways of dealing with all the personal belongings. There are no formulas. Some people need to hang on longer than others. When I gave Leonard's clothes away, I got help from his daughter and son-in-law. Help helps. Don't be afraid to ask for it. I once worked with a widow who would not change anything in her husband's closet. She even left his hat in the exact spot where he had always left it, saying she didn't think he'd want her to move it. Her denial hardened as she clung to her fantasy that her husband would "return." We worked together for almost eight months before she was able to let go of the relationship enough to acknowledge the reality that he would never come back.

There are no formulas or timetables for after-death activities. Certainly there are no formulas or timetables for feelings that are part of these activities. However, I think a good question to ask yourself is whether your actions are helping you move forward or helping you stay where you are. Clothes kept as they were may make you feel as if life is still the way it was. Like Vera, like my patient, and like me, you need to acknowledge that it is not.

Vera listened to our versions of her struggle and, in several cases, our resolutions. "Tell me," she seemed to be saying, "but please don't push me. Let me know how you managed it, but don't expect me to move too quickly." We understood. Mourning is a process, not an isolated action or event. She, like us, would need time, time to let go.

And every week we fought with loneliness. Ironically Cliff felt his most acutely when he was with his daughter: his intense connection with her was isolating him from the rest of the world. But Vera's anxiety attacks occurred only when she was alone. She insisted she heard the sound of silence. Norman's fear of his anger reinforced his lack of social skills, which made him feel increasingly isolated. In my case, I was fine only when I was working. It was working that gave me structure: having to get up, having to get dressed, having to get a move on. Also, it connected me to people. Nights and weekends I felt powerless, powerless and disconnected. If I was alone I felt diminished. Sometimes I felt as if I didn't even exist, as if I needed others to reinforce the reality of me. Still I thought I was managing better than the others—in the group, I was sure I was composed and helpful. My rudest shock occurred after only four meetings. I remarked, as I supposed I had before, that I still couldn't understand the desertion of some of my friends—why was there no one special with whom I could share the desolation of my times alone?

Norman, far from my favorite among the half dozen of us, turned on me, his heavy face coloring above the bulge of his collar: "When the hell are you going to cut this shit? We're getting sick of all your whining! Aren't you supposed to be a therapist? Maybe it's time you started trying to cure yourself instead of staying so sickeningly stuck."

I was hurt—staggered—by this perception of me. On the way home I was furious. Surely I had been no more of a wimp than anyone else. And what was the group for but support anyway? There was no way I'd return.

A week later, over my infantile rage, I went back, rather meekly determined to get unstuck.

One other group storm precipitated itself over Cliff. He announced one day that without having said anything to his clinging daughter, he had joined a singles club. When she found out that he had a "date" lined up and another in the offing, all hell broke loose over "How could you do this to Mother?" All hell broke loose in the group when we heard about it too—we jumped on Cliff for his selfishness; after all, his daughter was right: it *had* only been six months. But by the end of the session we gave him our blessing, recognizing that if he didn't make such an attempt at change, he and that kid could be living together for years to come in that same old stifling togetherness.

Betsy, on the other hand, maintained that she wasn't having any trouble with being alone. Every time she spoke, it was with the voice of an authority who had resolved all her feelings. I wondered why she was in the group; she seemed almost tranquil. But one day her defenses collapsed. She was talking about her certainty that her husband had fallen, not jumped, off the boat. Cliff then said he didn't think anybody in a marriage knew for certain what his or her mate was feeling. He was focusing on the secrets even happy couples kept from each other. The group agreed. Suddenly there was a threat that all these so-called perfect relationships could be looked at more honestly. We were both repelled and attracted to the idea. Betsy got up, threatening to leave, then quickly sat down. "Maybe," she said slowly, "maybe I should stay." We all suddenly saw tears form: the Betsy who couldn't cry was crying.

How we all want to idealize and idolize our lost mates! If the marriage has been perfect, we don't have to deal with guilt, guilt caused by negative feelings toward our spouse. Widows in my practice usually begin talking about themselves as being part of a "golden couple." It feels so much safer than dealing with ambivalence. But ambivalence doesn't destroy. Once you are able to accept it, it can be used as a mobilizing force. Mixed feelings are part of all relationships when people are alive. Why can't they still exist when one person dies?

For a while in the group it looked as if every member had been married to a saint. We had not. As we began to accept this reality—the good parts of our marriage as well as those we wished could have been better—we found ourselves moving on to a healthier place, and I found I had stopped feeling sick and crazy.

The group offered the right help for me and was my first experience with group therapy. I found myself comparing it to my personal and professional experience with individual therapy. Because of its numbers, a group echoes the voices of support and sharing by contributing the strength of many people recognizing your predicament. Drug users have the highest rate of success in helping other addicts, alcoholics form the foundation of the successful AA, and widows help widows.

The group was a new and compelling experience for me: the sharing; my questions answered by other people's solutions to similar problems; multiple challenges from people who lovingly insisted that I move forward.

Widows have often asked me the advantage of individual therapy. Individual therapy, I've explained, can help you explore your history of loss. For example, how did you handle previous deaths? Is there still unfinished business that torments you? Leftover baggage can create intolerable guilt. The way you handled early losses will very much dictate how you handle your loss now. Also, you find new ways to explore and resolve old feelings.

But both individual and group therapy can help. Unfortunately not every community offers one comparable to my Manhattan group—New Images for the Widowed, run by Pat Bertrand. If you are unable to find a group, think about the possibility of starting one yourself. I had a patient who moved to Trinidad after her husband died. For months she tried to find a bereavement group with whom she could share her feelings of loss. Finally she placed an ad in the Trinidad newspaper, talked to people in her church, and was able to find nine people who joined her group.

Starting your own group might sound like an overwhelming concept if you live in Tulsa, Tacoma, East Lansing, or in a small town, but file it away among your options. There is the National Self-Help Clearing House in New York that gives referrals for groups throughout the country. Their address is 25 West Forty-third Street, Room 620, New York, N.Y. 10036, and their telephone number is (212) 642–2944. If they can't help you, you can run an ad in your local paper and talk to your church or club members. You don't need a professional social worker or psychotherapist to lead a group. Once the original timidity and stiffness have lessened, groups have a way of running themselves.

Do all widows need group or individual therapy? Most of us can benefit from one or the other or both. There may be exceptions, but all therapies offer help with the feelings of isolation. Counseling of some sort can be a turning point, whichever route you take. Individual therapy helps resolve past conflicts; group therapy fortifies your coping skills. Both will help you stop feeling crazy and chaotic, and both will help you deal with the emerging you—the return to the loving self.

5

Life Is What Happens While You're Making Other Plans

Getting through It so You Can Get on with It

It's easy enough to put together a list of mourning clichés: "Time heals." "Don't think about the past, think about the future." "What's over is over." "Pull yourself together." And my all-time favorite, "It's time to get on with your life."

This last suggestion was made to me when the decision about whether or not to get out of bed felt major. What to wear, what to eat, how to get from one place to another were all challenges. The people who were talking about my moving forward might just as well have been speaking Mandarin—I simply didn't understand. I still had an intense need to talk through and share my memories. I talked obsessively about Leonard, especially his last months in the hospital, reliving, picturing, describing each incident. It was as if by doing so I was testing my relationship's reality and at the same time the reality of its loss. I continued to be plagued by anniversaries of events, recent and past. I found myself filled with intense pain on the day of the week or month that was the day Leonard had died. The first anniversary of his death was particularly hard; I relived it in its entirety that day as well as on those that immediately followed it.

Many widows have told me that they have gotten anniversary reactions for many years after their husband's death. One widow told me that as the anniversary day approached she would feel as if she had fallen behind a stone wall. She would feel alone and lost and totally cut off from the people around her, although she had been consciously unaware that the anniversary of his death was coming. It was only *after* the anniversary date passed that she recognized the connection between the day and her feelings.

After four years of this she decided to deal directly with the anniversary instead of having it "'sneak up" on her. At the beginning of the anniversary month she began writing notes to herself: "Be careful, it's coming! Don't forget that you get crazy every year. Don't overlook it." And later, "Watch out! Only three days left." On the "day," taking extra good care of herself, she went to the hairdresser and to an aerobics class, and planned a special evening with her daughter and son-in-law who were taking her to a new play. It turned out to be a much easier day than it had been over the past few years.

But of course it's not only anniversaries that are so difficult. At the same time I was dealing with my "firsts"—my first birthday, my first spring, summer, Christmas, even my first drive alone to a friend's house, all the first times for me alone, without Leonard. Some of my friends supported me in this bonding review; others, because of their own anxieties about death, were unable to do so.

"Can't you talk about anything else?" one asked. "No, I can't," I answered, knowing I wasn't ready. I felt as if I were being governed by an internal alarm clock that hadn't completed its run. My friends were in a hurry to put an end to my mourning. Luckily I knew better than to let them.

This push from friends who are ahead of our mourning is understandable, but it needs to be monitored carefully by you. You need to go through whatever the process is for *you*. Don't use other people's schedules or accept their plans for ending your mourning, because their way could result in an amputation rather than a resolution.

Elsa, a forty-five-year-old patient of mine, makes a good case in point of how well-intentioned advice can sabotage mourning. Elsa's husband, Curt, was killed when his car skidded on a slippery road. The police came to Elsa with the news and asked if she would identify the body. Elsa wanted to go, but her friend Ann and her mother went instead, telling Elsa that she should not see the body; it would only upset her. She should, her mother insisted, remember Curt as he was.

In the days that followed, more friends appeared. They advised her not to think about the past, only to think about the future. Whenever Elsa brought up her concerns about how Curt had died, she was told not to think about it because "he couldn't have suffered anything." She wanted desperately to talk about it for many reasons, but especially because the night before the accident she and Curt had argued about money, which she now felt had agitated him enough to cause the accident. No one would let her express her feelings of guilt. Each time she tried to do so, she was told she had been "the best wife," and that there was nothing for her to feel bad about.

Elsa was also experiencing anger at Curt for leaving her. She couldn't understand this feeling but every time she tried to explore it with friends or relatives, they became very uncomfortable, changing the subject quickly and telling her not to upset herself. Her mother told her that if she let herself feel angry she would be unable to cope with anything. When Elsa wanted to cry, especially at night when she missed Curt the most, her mother and friends reminded her of how lucky she was—she had had a wonderful husband and had a terrific fifteen-year-old daughter who, if she saw her mother cry, would be doubly hurt.

Curt had been dead nine months before Elsa was referred to me by an internist who could find no physical cause for her significant weight loss of thirty pounds over a six-month period. Elsa's loss of appetite was accompanied by burning pains in her chest, back, and abdomen, which she was convinced indicated a fatal abdominal cancer. She was withdrawn and isolated, unable to move, uninterested in family and friends, and unresponsive to their attempts to make her feel better. She awakened at four every morning and was unable to go back to sleep. She claimed to feel worst in the morning, improving slightly as the day wore on.

Elsa spoke to me about her feelings of extreme unworthiness and commented that death from cancer would be a blessing. The only mention of Curt came when she asked self-consciously whether I thought she was "crazy" because she continued to have lengthy conversations with his photograph, which she kept by her bed. The content of these talks, she said, was primarily about her guilt over their money fight the night before the accident.

Elsa was suffering from melancholia. Her friends and family had failed her by not accepting her feelings, not being able to deal with them. Despite their well-intentioned efforts, these people were inadequate in the face of Elsa's major trauma. Like all widows she needed permission to talk about everything—positive and negative feelings, fears, questions, doubts, all unfinished business. Elsa was blocked and stuck because the people around her had stopped her mourning process.

Elsa was in treatment for six months before she began slowly to gain weight. We had to start at the beginning of her conflict, allowing her to express all of the feelings she had repressed and displaced onto herself. Physical symptoms and fears about dying began to fade, although they still plagued her occasionally. I felt she needed more support and exploration than she was getting from individual therapy and referred her to a group for the widowed, which helped her work with me enormously. Little by little she relived the trauma of Curt's death by going through her terror and desperation, her anger and guilt, her anxiety and despair—and gradually she was able to let go. Her once-truncated mourning was well on its way to completion.

Elsa, like the rest of us, had gone in circles. Setbacks, recurrences, forward, sideways, and backward: straight lines in mourning do not occur. But no matter how circuitous the route taken, we all find ourselves in a different place from where we started. The old self has gone with your old life and, much as you want that self back, it will never return. We are not what we were either before or during our marriage. Now we're in transition, challenging our past structure, raising questions, exploring possibilities. Each transition leads to termination of a previous life structure. It has been said that there is no loss that cannot lead to gain. No one can handle that concept without the recognition that, given a choice, they would forgo the loss. Life, unfortunately, doesn't offer that choice.

It took six months before I began to feel new energy to invest in the world outside myself. I was coming back to life in very small ways. I stopped in my lobby to play with a small child, feeling her spontaneity and warmth. Then one of my friends said to me one night after a dinner party, "You're going to be fine. I knew it when I heard you laugh." And most of all, *I* knew I was coming back when I realized, with the sharp focus of surprise—and yes, some guilt too— that I hadn't thought about Leonard for an entire day.

I was being forced to rethink my life and see if past choices still worked. Did I want to continue being a therapist in private practice, which is an isolated way to work? Or did I need the stimulation and social contact found in a hospital or psychiatric institution? I even wondered about being a therapist at all. What if, I mused, I wanted—one more time—to change careers altogether? In one of my more infantile moments, I thought about joining the Peace Corps so I could pick up and start my life over in a foreign country, carrying all my possessions in a duffel bag.

What would I actually do if I completely changed my life? Before marriage I had been a researcher for a television network, working for Chet Huntley; later I was a part-time writer. Did I want to rekindle those interests and see if such activities still excited me?

I searched back through the years looking for the me before I was married, wondering where my capable alone self was hiding. Did I leave it behind when I married? No, I decided, I was a three-part amalgamation—the me before, the me during, and the me after Leonard. If I could only figure out how to utilize all three of these parts.

My exploration into professional options ended with the revelation of how lucky I was to be doing the work I loved. Many widows are not so fortunate. Either for economic reasons, or for ways to keep busy, or for ways of meeting people, widows need to work. If you haven't been working throughout your marriage, you may have to start at the beginning. I know a widow, married when she was eighteen, who had never worked a day in her life. But she convinced a potential employer that her many years as a homemaker had trained her perfectly to help him run his decorating business. She was hired with no "job experience," because she had proudly asserted her talent and willingness to learn.

Usually it is harder. Even if you worked years ago, it is difficult to reenter the job market. Many widows find a way into the professional world by working as a volunteer. Others discover they need additional education before they can get the job they want.

All of these decisions are individual and depend on specific circumstances, but my experience with widows is that they are often unaware of talents they have and, given time, guts, and letting people know of their availability, do far better than they expected.

In my case, I would think about Leonard's preferences and how he would have dealt with a particular problem, but at the same time I was aware that my life was going on without him. I had not only survived the first year, I was making decisions that normally would have been shared but were now my responsibilities for which I alone would take the consequences.

My professional life was happening even if my social life was in shambles. Among our couple friends I was definitely the odd one out, eliciting a strong response from them somewhere between amazement that I was still alive and functioning, and acute discomfort. Oh, how I hated being called a widow, and even worse, *the* widow. People didn't look at me when they said "widow," and even hearing the word on the telephone made me feel as if I weren't there.

Facing the first time I went to a party alone was so anxiety-provoking that I failed to realize its importance. Everything felt new and uncomfortable, but symbolically I had seen the dragon with fire in its nose and had dealt with it and lived to talk about it. I knew my solo status was making my friends uncomfortable. If we were to continue to be friends, we would need to find ways to reconnect, since our old patterns of interaction no longer worked.

Society is oriented to couples and rarely takes the trouble to deal with widows. People send mixed messages: on the one hand they say shape up, don't whine, be brave, be competent. On the other hand they expect us to maintain our grief-stricken, paralyzed position because it will keep us segregated from their world. We are forced to find ourselves by ourselves. It seems an overwhelming task, but it gets easier as you acknowledge your potential for growth. I'm reminded of the time, many years ago, when I broke my arm. In the process of healing it developed a new protective covering that made it stronger than my other bones. Like my arm, we widows heal with additional strength after our mourning is completed.

After going to that first party alone I still had difficulties to get through before I could "get on" with my life, but now I knew what the phrase meant. Like a car stuck in snow, I inched forward, then backward, again and again not noticing that each inch forward edged me a little ahead of the place I had been before.

Where to Live with the Loneliness

Loneliness has a sound. I heard it for the first time when I returned home the night Leonard was hospitalized. It was a dark, hollow sound that echoed with sobs of abandonment. I was reminded of my childhood in a New York apartment over an alley where cats yowled through the night. "Mommy," I asked once, "are those kids down there who are lost? Could we help them?" She explained that they weren't children but alley cats. Despite her explanation, the sound haunted me for years.

How this new void reverberated through the house. He was never going to be here again—never! It was Leonard's house, somehow much more than mine, and for many reasons: it had been his choice not to live in the city, his need for the privacy of a house rather than an apartment, his love for each special object purchased on his tours around the world. "Why will he never come back?" the house moaned. I had no answer.

Over the following weeks and months I heard the sound intermittently. It had never been at the hospital even as his condition worsened, but it was in the house, my car, going to and from work, and it was especially loud at meals. I had been eating alone comfortably for years, since Leonard traveled so much; I had never before given it a thought. Now it became a chore. I managed with difficulty to eat at home but eating in restaurants was intolerable. Food tasted like medicine as I heard the faint, sad moan of loneliness.

In addition my body felt bruised, every bone aching, as if I had fallen from a great height. I wanted to protect it, but it demanded a soothing warmth. Inside a mature woman, a lost child needed to snuggle. When I was in graduate school

I half kiddingly informed Leonard that the stresses of school were causing a major regression—I felt like sucking my thumb. Leonard bought me a stuffed rabbit, which I slept with until graduation. Now "Bunny" was retrieved from the closet shelf and put to sleep in Leonard's place, helping me to deal with the intense loneliness caused by the loss of my best friend.

Bunny became so important that I even took to talking to it. "Bunny," I said, "needing you so much makes me feel like a crazy mess."

My loneliness was overwhelming. "Two by two, marching into the ark," I said to myself as I sadly watched the rest of the world go by. "Everyone is part of a pair except me." "Nonsense," responded my rational self, "you're seeing things because you are feeling lost and raw." But loneliness won over rationality; I continued to see a universe of couples.

I read an article about a loon living on a lake in Maine. When her mate died, she too died, because loons are unable to survive without their mates. I wondered if it was the same with human beings. It was a terrifying thought.

A widowed friend allowed her son-in-law's sister to spend a month in her one-bedroom apartment. She had told me previously about her intense dislike for the sister and when I asked her why she was letting her share her limited space, said, "Anything and anyone is better than no one. She at least breaks the silence."

Another widow left her TV on when she went to work each morning because she couldn't bear to walk into a silent house. She insisted that silence made the room seem dark no matter how many lights she turned on.

Not too long ago I would have pointed out that she wasn't making a lot of sense, but now I knew exactly what she

meant. I had thought of myself as one of those postlibera-
tion women who reveled in doing her own thing, being her
own person, and delighting in her *me*-generation attitude.
What ever happened to my partially accepted feminist approach? I rummaged through my close relationships with
feminist friends whose liberated stances had both intrigued
and scared me. Their free, creative, unconventional pose
very much appealed to me, but their strident position that
men should be little more than tolerated went against my
deep affection and respect for men. What would my feminist friends say now about my desperate feelings of loneliness, I asked myself, almost afraid to find out.

My need and curiosity overcame the fear. I called a close
friend and colleague who had strongly influenced me over
the years.

Her position had hardened since our previous discussion—hardened to the point where we were completely
polarized: north/south, right/wrong, black/white. The conversation made me feel as if we were strangers. Her mili-
tance was overwhelming. "Be grateful," she said directly,
"you're alone and don't have to negotiate with anyone else.
Your time is your own, your space and possessions are
untouched and you can do what you want."

What I wanted, I told her, was Leonard and the life we
had had together. She pushed me further, incredulous that
I could fail to see my advantage over her and others stuck
with undeserving and demanding men. I was the chosen
one who no longer had to put up with a husband's
demands—with buying food and cooking, or doing boring
chores, going to the dry cleaners, having to answer his telephone calls and take down his messages.

I was struck by her vehemence; she was truly filled with
hate. Even through my fog of loneliness I heard an angry,

bitter woman for whom only a solitary existence would alleviate a marital disease. We tried to continue our discussion a little longer, talking for over an hour until I found I couldn't talk to her anymore. She advised me to see a therapist and wound up the conversation with "Work on yourself, you've lost it."

I had already decided to consult a therapist, not for the reasons she had suggested, but for help with all my unanswered questions and incomplete exploration of my feelings. "Physician, heal thyself" did not work for me, nor had it worked for the remarkable, twice-widowed therapist I was lucky enough to find. Her response to my loneliness was acutely different from that of my feminist friend. She helped me examine the differences between my need for healthy nurturing, mirroring, reinforcement, sharing, and loving, and my neurotic, infantile unfinished business. She reinforced the healthy, lonely feelings, promising correctly that they would fade as time passed and would to a great extent disappear as I made new connections and began to grow. After we discussed my friend's euphoria over the single state versus the married state, my therapist quoted her hero Martin Buber, who said all real living is a meeting between I and Thou, and that "through the Thou a person becomes I."

When I told her I needed to know that someone cared whether I lived or died, she pointed out that I already knew several people who clearly did. "Take some of your energy," she wisely suggested, "and connect more forcefully with those people."

My feelings of loneliness were so overpowering that at first I couldn't find the necessary energy. I asked my therapist if I would have been as lonely if I had had children. She showed me a study of widows with and without children that found that while children need and constantly stay with their widowed mothers, and are a source of love and attachment, they fail to diminish a widow's sense of loneliness. Nor in the same study did friends help alleviate loneliness in the early stages of mourning.

Together we worked our way through this period of profound isolation. We examined the dictates of modern society: the necessity to strive for and to value our self-sufficiency, our self-reliance, and our self-containment—to know, if by necessity or by choice, we can survive alone.

I recalled my work with patients on this problem, done over many years in my practice. The joining of their different selves—one independent, sufficient, highly functioning separate entity, the other more dependent, needy, child-like, and wishing to connect and be part of a pair. My patients had tended to choose the either/or route, causing them many problems until they discovered it was the blending of both selves that always worked for them.

Now I was asking both of *my* selves why it wasn't working for me. If either one had answered it would have told me my pervasive loneliness had frozen my capacity to think.

Loneliness affects all widows. It is intrusive and controlling; it can dominate our actions and our thoughts. We make mistakes that, without its crushing, numbing effect, we would never otherwise make. I thought of Frances, the friend of a friend, a widow of two months, who had lived with her husband in Bel-Air, California, for over thirty years. Her forty-year-old daughter, Sylvia, persuaded her to move from California to a small town in Virginia where the daughter and her husband and their two children lived.

Frances found herself relying on her daughter and son-in-law for everything. She lived in an apartment near them but was limited to their family schedules and their decisions as to when they would see her. Without a car, she never went anywhere or met new people on her own. Sylvia, living an established life in the community with friends and a part-time job, showed mixed feelings about her mother's move, even though she had been the one who urged her to do so. One minute she talked about her joy at having a "grandmother" close by and a central part of their lives. At other times she complained bitterly to friends about being responsible for and burdened by her mother.

Mother and daughter began to fight when Frances, feeling increasingly dependent, asked for more time with the children. Sylvia rejected the idea, arguing that it wasn't good for young children to spend too much time with an unhappy adult, adding that she wanted her mother to stop talking about her father, thereby cutting off Frances's recovery before it began. Sylvia issued other ultimatums, including the times at which her mother could telephone the family and what Frances should do to occupy her time: Sylvia thought it was appropriate for her to take courses at the local college but not to involve herself in charity work. The arguments increased in direct proportion to both the mother's and daughter's conflict about their dependence. Frances, three thousand miles from her old home without a connection other than Sylvia, found herself in a more hurtful situation than the period directly following her husband's death. She assumed her unbearable pain was caused only by her recent loss when in fact the daughter was a major factor.

Sylvia, out of touch with her own feelings of loss, had evicted her mother from her familiar, structured, comfortable world. She has been unable to say to Frances, "Please come live with us. I miss Dad so much and having you live with us will make it better." Instead, under the guise of caring and support, she had offered her mother an isolated, truncated, solitary life. Frances, because she was so lonely, accepted, assuming anything would be better than living alone in her house in Bel-Air.

It took Frances a year before she accepted defeat. Her relationship with her daughter was in shambles, which precluded any healthy rewarding relationship with her grandchildren. She could talk only with her son-in-law, who weakly acknowledged his wife's hostility but offered no solutions.

Frances knew she had to find a way back to her life, a life where she could pick up the process that had stopped when she moved. Stoically she studied her options and alternatives, focusing on places to live where she had friends and where there would be opportunities for new experiences. She decided to return to California, where she rented an apartment near her old house. She had come home to a life that felt far less lonely than it had felt before she left. She had benefited from her mistake of moving too quickly and without thought. She had learned a major lesson. She had been lonelier living with "family" than she had been living alone but surrounded by loving friends.

Frances had fought and made the right decision. All widows fight the same battle in different places and in different ways. The dictum "Don't make any major changes in your life for at least a year" is sound advice, but I didn't follow it. I made a major change, moving to the city from our house in the suburbs five months after Leonard died, and it proved to be an absolutely right decision. It was based on my long-term desire to live in the city, which had been set aside in favor of Leonard's great wish to live in the country.

Past preferences made my resolution of the debate about country versus city living easy. You may find that the problem of where to live—whether to move or stay—can be disturbing, since it involves painful adjustment. Some widows feel the need to move very quickly after their loss. Others do not. I know one woman who, three months after her husband died, rented her house to friends because her memories of her husband and their life in the house were too harsh—every object, every piece of furniture, reminded her of their joint life. She felt as if she were living with a ghost whose presence overpowered her. So for a year she rented an apartment and slowly discovered how much she missed her house and belongings. After the year was over, she returned to the familiar surroundings of her old home.

There are two sides to the coin. If you remain in your house you may need to find help with the everyday problems—dripping faucets, running toilets, leaf-filled gutters, and other minutiae your husband once took care of. But on the other hand your house is yours alone, with privacy and tranquillity hard to find in an apartment. Your house is comfortable and your neighborhood familiar.

Money will, of course, be a major consideration. Moving versus staying, an apartment versus a house, are all options that must be considered in relation to your financial picture. Ask as many questions of others—accountant, banker, lawyer—as you need to.

Since we are all products of our unique pasts, what works for one of us may not work for others. Many of my friends were deeply shocked by my quick decision—they hadn't known of my preferences during all the years I lived outside the city, nor did they take into account the six-month period during Leonard's long illness I had had to think about what lay ahead.

Friends think they know what's best for you, what you

should and shouldn't do. You probably assume that everyone else knows better than you do what is right for you. You're wrong; they don't. You know a lot more than they do, but until you're able to get in touch with what you know, just *be!* Don't move or not move because someone tells you to do so or not. Above all, remember that you are allowed to make a mistake. Like Frances, you can go home again, and like me you can make a decision early that works. As another widow once said to me, "Pencils wouldn't have erasers if we didn't make mistakes."

Traveling on Your Own

The trouble with going away is coming home. People don't take this paradox into account when they tell you to take a trip, go somewhere, get away, see a new world! It's an unexplored rule; widows travel if they're fortunate enough to have the time and the money. It's one of those activities we're *supposed* to undertake.

Advice is easier than action. People mean well; traveling is something they'd want to do, so they're sure we'd like it too. We're sent away by benevolent people, often before we're ready to go.

To start with, if we are used to our husbands making arrangements, are we ready to take full responsibility, are we ready to do it ourselves? Sure, we say, we're adults, and besides, there's always a travel agent who can make all the concrete arrangements. So if we have the time and the money, what could cause a problem?

We're causing the problem, we with our questions about how to travel alone in a foreign country where we know no one. Some of us, through our professional lives, are familiar with solitary travel. I wasn't, and like me, many of you haven't traveled alone since before you were married. Youth made travel a playful adventure. Now it's a serious one. Others tell us that it can serve as a turning point. They're right—it can be an astonishing break in our routinized life. But if we're still anxious in our safe and familiar homes, how will we feel in unknown places with all those intriguing new people? Travel seems like a courageous maneuver indeed.

Should we or shouldn't we go? If we do, should it be to a foreign place or somewhere closer to home? How much should it cost? For how long should it be? Is it possible actually to go it entirely alone?

I for one had massive doubts about my first solo trip. Leonard had scheduled a concert tour of China just before his illness canceled it. Having done my homework, I had been looking forward intensely to the trip and now, eighteen months later, was making it on my own. I knew it wouldn't be the same but I hoped to love it and to learn new things, meet interesting people, and return home refreshed and improved.

My departure filled me with ambivalence and separation anxiety. Two days before we were to leave, Libya blew up a U.S. jetliner. We retaliated with a bombing attack. They then threatened to retaliate against our retaliation. At that point I tried to cancel my trip, but the tour guide informed me that it was too late for a refund. My fears percolated. I was convinced I'd never come back and that no one would miss me or even take notice. I ruminated about impending disasters, both cosmic and personal—my apartment would be flooded, the entire United States would be bombed. Even my carry-on luggage seemed filled with apprehension as I staggered reluctantly to the plane.

My anxieties were not totally unfounded: planes in China almost never arrive or depart on schedule. I didn't see my suitcase for days at a time; luggage in China remains a national mystery. I became physically exhausted from the demanding schedule—out at dawn, to bed at midnight. But I also felt intoxicated by a world completely different from anything I'd experienced before. I was able to hook myself into a new and invigorating culture; being in Shanghai made me feel as if I'd wandered right into a 1947 movie, and having Peking duck in Peking gave me a major kick. I was acutely aware of my positive, free, happy feelings, juxtaposed against my loneliness and sadness about not being able to share the excitement. What would Leonard have thought about it? I constantly wondered.

I watched the five couples in my group relate and interact with one another in ways I envied. The couples, another widow, and I—"the group, the gang, the clan," as we called ourselves—were a solid, interesting mixture of diverse ages from different places. I was somewhere in the middle of the age range and felt comfortable with everyone. My only bleak moment each day was the five o'clock slump, when the couples retired to their rooms to review the day's activities. It felt terrible; where was my co-reviewer? Joan, the other widow, and I made the decision to meet in the hotel bar at five to do our own reviewing. During the day we saw the wonders of China and together we compared notes, shopped, and shared the lives we'd left in the United States. At the same time I was aware both that Leonard was not with me and that I was having a good time.

Two powerful opposing feelings coexisted as I discovered a sense of competency traveling. Before, I'd been taken care of when I traveled. Leonard was the traveler and I was along for the ride.

Sally, a patient of mine, talked about her fear of taking a trip to Virginia for the first time after her husband died. When they traveled, he had always done the packing for her as well as for himself, an act that was symbolic of their thirty-year marriage. He was the kindly, avuncular figure packing for a little-girl wife. Sally, unaware she was meeting his need to be needed, honestly believed she was unable to pack for herself. Within the framework of their marriage this arrangement worked: she played helpless child and he played Uncle Macho, until one day Uncle died, leaving Sally feeling incompetent about everything—symptomatically about packing.

Her sense of helplessness showed up in her dreams; she dreamed she was trapped in a burning building, in a wheelchair, being pushed down a flight of stairs. Her most recent dream was about being on an ocean liner and not being allowed in the dining room because she had nothing to wear. Finally, encouraged by me, Sally told her daughter about her packing phobia. The daughter, sensing the depth of her mother's problem, reversed roles with her and, parenting Sally, taught her exactly how to pack a bag. Though packing seemed like a small action, at the same time it was a powerful impediment.

Sally made the trip to Virginia to see her family and shortly afterward went on a cruise with friends. About a year later, she took an entry-level job with a consulting firm and moved quickly to a level that required traveling to associated companies. Packing was no longer a concern.

Jan, a widowed friend who had traveled only with her husband, was terrified at the prospect of taking a trip. However, pressured by another friend, she agreed to make arrangements to go to the Grand Canyon, which she had always wanted to see. Upon their arrival Jan realized she had neglected to reserve a hotel room. She panicked and began crying for her husband. He would have known better, he would have thought ahead, he would have had the room. When she calmed down, she called every hotel in the directory, finally locating one with a cancellation.

Jan knew that she had won a major battle. Enjoying more than the reality of finding a room, she reveled in her new sense of competency and control over her environment.

Jan, Sally, and I all received multiple benefits from traveling. But for me, coming home was another matter. My life in New York had been left on a back burner simmering away, and I returned from China to confront all the unresolved pieces that I had left three weeks before. Even the actual homecoming—walking into the apartment and not having anyone to greet me—made everything seem drab and strange. Coming home alone felt like an ending to a unique experience—the shutting off of an expansion-in-progress. I felt as if I were moving backward. Being away had anesthetized my anxiety and dimmed life's realities. Coming home meant picking up unfinished drudgery—the accumulated estate issues, legal hassles, battles with insurance companies over payment of medical bills. It also meant continued exploration of my options and more resolutions to unanswered questions. On the return flight I sadly regretted the loss of structure: a schedule determined by others, shared meals, a predetermined daily life. At home I would be in charge of me again.

It was a challenge, but somehow I felt better equipped to face it; the China experience had strengthened and added to my armament.

When widows ask me for my views on travel, I recall my own feelings of vitality and competence, but need at the same time to point out that all travel experiences are unique.

My own was successful because of the timing, the fortunate mix of people, and the exotic places I was able to explore. Many widows have different reactions—they talk about their despair and isolation when they've traveled alone or with an uncongenial and unsympathetic traveling companion. I hear tales from women who feel abandoned by their children who "send them away," more for their own gain than for their mother's needs.

Dana, a friend, went on a cruise four months after her husband died. Her daughter and son-in-law told her, "This is the perfect time for you to go and get your act together. Do it before you have to deal with all the unhappy stuff." They knew she would soon have to close up her big house that had become a burden and look for a more appropriate place in which to live. Dana was not emotionally prepared to go anywhere. Overcome with shyness, she remained in her stateroom alone for most of the trip, including mealtimes, feeling more isolated and frightened than she would have felt had she stayed at home and begun to live her new life. Not dealing with her problems fed directly into her sense of inadequacy and fears for the future.

Carol, a widow of eight months, told me about a trip she had taken with old dear friends who, without telling her, had invited another widowed friend to join them on their trip through the English countryside. The two widows shared a room. Carol was unhappy with her roommate; with each new day she became increasingly depressed without knowing why. The other widow was completely harmless and inoffensive. Carol couldn't figure out what was bothering her until, with a jolt, she realized that it was the first time in thirty years that she had shared a room with anyone other than her husband. She recognized that her discomfort had to do only with her loss, not with the other widow. From that realization on, her depression began to lift.

You may decide that you are getting enough new experiences right at home—after all, you're negotiating your way through a foreign land even without opening your front door. And the more comfortable you become with yourself, regardless of where you are, the more you'll eventually enjoy new places, new people, and new experiences.

My skin felt comfortable in China, but when I came home, once more it felt pulled and constricted. You may want to avoid traveling until you know that coming home will be a comfortable experience, unlike mine. Whatever you decide, you should stay aware that, like life itself, travel (the timing, the place, the people) is a great big gamble for everyone, not just for widows.

On the other hand, most widows end up feeling that the positive aspects of traveling are far greater than the negative ones. The probability is that you will be meet new and interesting people. Remember, you will be meeting people who didn't know you as part of a couple; they will be meeting you as the unique individual that you are.

6

What to Expect

Weekend Hospitality

Penny, widowed for a year, was referred to me by a divorced patient for help with her social life. Penny described herself as being "stuck between a rock and a hard place" because she hated being either with couples or with other unattached women. Being with both groups left her feeling intensely segregated despite their willingness to include her. In the months immediately following her husband's death she had been socially active with both couples and single friends, but now she was choosing to stay home alone every night. Increasingly depressed, she refused to call anyone because she was afraid that they'd want to make a date.

We debated her conflict: why was she so unfulfilled by every social transaction? Historically she had been a social being, moving easily through life's transitions, surrounded by friends. Now she felt paralyzed.

I knew exactly how Penny felt, recalling a dilemma of my own that was symbolized by two specific weekends during my first summer alone. I had been delighted to be asked to spend a weekend in Bucks County by my old and good friends Maggie and David, who said, "Come on Friday and stay as long as you like." I could come and go as I pleased, eat when and whatever I wanted—in short, I would be free to do my own thing. The pool would be mine to use as freely as everything else in the house.

What they failed to mention, however, was that they were heavily involved in a major feud with each other. They also overlooked their unmentioned expectation that I would be their mediator. Unknown to me, and perhaps on an unconscious level unknown to them, they were looking for a third party to take them out of themselves and away from each other—my presence was to provide a new and challenging focus. Clinically this is called triangulation. Non-clinically it's called undeclared war.

I arrived in time for supper, which I brought with me. Maggie and David greeted me warmly and the food more so, since neither had been willing to shop. Maggie explained that this was a long-standing issue between them, both holding firmly to their stance that it was the other's responsibility. As he unpacked the food, David asked me questions about my life in New York, but before I could answer Maggie interrupted, suggesting we have a round of drinks. The tension between them thickened as we drank and it wasn't till ten that we sat down to dinner. By then Maggie and David were screaming at each other.

According to Maggie, David was neglecting their relationship by not communicating with her about "feelings." David said he was sick to death of discussing their relationship; all he wanted was to *have* it, not just *talk about it* all the time. Maggie produced a list of complaints she had put together the previous week, detailing the extent of David's obsession with Wall Street. He retaliated by criticizing her for not keeping the house neat. Turning to me, Maggie challenged "someone" to defend the working woman. When I remained silent, David asked how many patients I worked with who flaunted traditional marital roles at their husbands' expense. Maggie's rage escalated; calling David a "chauvinistic shit," she turned to me for support, crying, "You'd better help now or he'll get you too!"

Paralyzed by my own despair, I couldn't say a word. My mind had gone back to picturing the four of us at parties, dinners, concerts. When Leonard became ill, Maggie and David had been totally supportive, visiting him daily in the hospital and helping me through the hardest of times. They seemed to have a solid, contented life together. Periodically they would argue, like most couples, but Leonard and I thought they related to each other in a hearty, joyous way. Two years before this night, they had bought their Bucks County house and with limitless energy quickly furnished it, naming it "Love Nest." From love nest to wasp's nest, I thought, as my stomach churned. Two halves of a couple who were alive, healthy, and vital—and determined to destroy each other and their relationship! Leukemia wouldn't kill David, but Maggie might.

They were both silent, waiting for me to join their struggle. I could barely whisper a peacemaking cliché before Maggie attacked *my* marriage, saying that my traditional marriage had robbed me of self-actualization. David joined in, declaring that Leonard had been too focused on his performing to encourage my growth. They smiled at each other after that one—they had found a new and safe victim.

In two seconds flat my despair turned to rage. How dare they criticize Leonard and our marriage! I exploded. Vodka and my yearning for Leonard obliterated my control. I told them to lay off me and Leonard and to take a long look at their careless treatment of each other, that they should treasure every moment they had together instead of yammering away. They were two ungrateful brats, I told them, who needed a kick in the pants.

Two pairs of eyes stared at me as two sets of ears shut down—it was if they had turned deaf. Back they went to attacking each other, Leonard, and our marriage. Now they had me in the ring and the fight was on. We stayed awake through the night debating relationships, love, sex, money, power, careers, entitlements. As the night wore on their marriage deteriorated.

At six-thirty in the morning David suggested breakfast, but by then my only interest was in sleep. A few hours later I awoke with my thoughts reordered. As I emerged from my room Maggie greeted me with the latest bulletin: David had agreed to get help to increase his sex drive, which somehow was repressed. David, looking like a beaten animal, headed outside to the garden to pull weeds, his favorite pastime. I resisted sharing my insight that it would be better for him to deal with Maggie, a more destructive weed than any in the garden. Instead I informed them that I had decided to return to the city.

Maggie immediately demanded to know why I wanted to leave. How could I do such a thing when we had all looked forward to the weekend so much? David, agreeing with her for the first time, insisted I stay, saying it would be good for all of us. He asked how I could choose the hot city over a weekend in their beautiful house in the country.

I excused myself by saying I probably wasn't good at being a weekend guest yet and would return later in the summer. Maggie launched into a speech about my owing them my presence in return for their support during Leonard's illness. I assured her I was grateful for that support and always would be, but couldn't offer myself as a referee in their fights. She accused me of "sanitizing" relationships by not dealing with the *real* issues. I'd had enough issues to last me a lifetime but I realized more talk at that point would be destructive. I suggested we talk later in the week and prepared to go.

"Stay!" she ordered. "If you value our friendship, stay!"

I assured her I valued it enormously but knew I had to leave. I needed fresh air—paradoxically, city air would feel clear and fresh compared to country air filled with hate and loathing. My home, lonely and empty, was now my refuge from destruction.

David saw me to my car, not saying a word. We looked at each other sympathetically and then hugged good-bye. I got into the car and drove back to the city with tears streaming down my face. They had it all, they had it all, but they were going to kill it.

My second traumatic couple weekend later that summer was diametrically opposite except for the fact that the invitation again came from old and close friends. Once more I arrived with supper, but this time I was greeted by two loving, nurturing, adoring people. Every word out of their mouths was prefaced by darling, sweetie, or honey. Harriet couldn't do enough to please Mark, and Mark hovered by her side waiting to meet her every wish or desire. If he went to the mailbox, he kissed her good-bye, and kissed her again on his return. When and what to eat, which movie she or he might like to see, to take or not to take a boat ride—these were subjects seriously discussed. They appeared to be joined at the hip—they moved together, cleaned together, gardened together, and talked endlessly together. They spoke always of "we," never "I."

Married twenty-six years, Harriet and Mark worshiped

each other, respected each other, and delighted in meeting each other's needs. Their *we*-ness was their shield against life's pain. (Each, protecting the other, was protected.) Looking at them sprawled out on the grass like innocent children, I felt a surge of melancholia—they had so much because they had each other. Nothing serious could penetrate their relationship. I remembered Leonard's saying that in the long run all that really mattered was us—together we could handle anything. Now I was seeing two people who had what we once had. They seemed so connected that I found it impossible to look at them without intolerable pain. Wistfully I recalled Leonard's once saying, when I had a toothache, that he couldn't believe it, but his mouth hurt too.

Now my melancholia turned to envy. It wasn't right, it wasn't fair. Why should they have it when we'd lost it? Why me? Why not her?

My resentments, which started as a trickle, became a flood. I told Harriet and Mark I wanted to go for a walk, but what I really wanted was to escape from their happiness.

As I walked my envy turned to suspicion. Nothing is that good, I sneered at the trees. They're too close; they're probably strangling each other. And what's underneath all the lovey-dovey stuff? What's it covering? For a minute I felt better. Perhaps it's a neurotic closeness, I thought; maybe they too are sad and unhappy. But the minute passed and I knew that what I'd witnessed was completely genuine— no act, no sham. If anything was being covered up underneath, it was even more intimate and intense feelings. I would have to live with my envy.

I'd like to say that by the time the weekend was over I'd gotten over my jealousy, but I hadn't. It took months before I was able to be with Harriet and Mark without feeling pain.

Fortunately we were a surviving threesome and to this day have stayed close. Many months later I was able to tell them how the first weekend with them had affected me. I was flabbergasted to discover they were aware of it and had attempted to decrease their affectionate interplay. As Mark aptly put it, it had been "a no-win situation."

Penny, describing herself as being between a rock and a hard place, was saying the same thing. Couples are potential land mines. If they hate each other, like Maggie and David, or love each other, like Harriet and Mark, they may attack precarious defenses on which we widowed depend so heavily. At the same time, couples have been a major source of our social pleasures. They are as different from unattached women (single, divorced, or widowed) as they are from one another.

Sometimes both groups seem to be more trouble than they're worth. Right? Wrong! More is healthy and less is lonely.

You need to accept weekend invitations both from couples and single people even if doing so makes you anxious and uncomfortable. It could turn out to be an experience similar to my two experiences, but it could also turn out to be very different. Not all couples are so extreme in their behavior, and getting away for a weekend can be a regenerative experience.

The "One Year" Myth

A widowed friend assured me that when Leonard had been dead for a year I would experience a radical change. She spoke of waking up on the morning of the exact day one year after her husband's death and feeling a sense of rebirth: an anniversary, an acknowledgment that the first year was over. She described in colorful detail her changes—a new bouncy step in her walk, a powerful ambition to clean closets and rearrange her kitchen, a desire to go shopping for new clothes, and her enactment of her fantasy of being a blonde. Out she went to have her hair cut and streaked—the new and released widow.

I was hoping a year after Leonard died to awaken with my version of renewal and excitement. Instead the day began and ended with pain and longing. I was filled with disappointment. Why hadn't my official one year of mourning ended?

As more months passed my disappointment turned to alarm—was there something seriously wrong with me? Instead of the positive changes I had been expecting, things felt even worse. I was sleeping less than during the first year, my concerns about physical symptoms were as vivid, and my social interactions had decreased. Fewer people were asking me away for the weekend, and couples were not including me as often as they had before. Friends had moved to phase two while I was stuck in phase one. My acute pain had diminished but at the same time my life hadn't concretely changed. I checked with my group and was relieved to find an even split—Cliff, Norman, and Vera had felt better after the first year ended, while Betsy, Sybil, and I thought the second year was harder in many ways. When I told this to a rabbi friend of mine, he suggested that we three were serious candidates for the term "pathological mourners."

I was stunned to find myself included in anything called pathological. Why was grief healthy up to a year and suddenly, after that, a sign of sickness? I talked to more people—therapists, the clergy, teachers—asking what's healthy and what is not. They all assured me that a year was appropriate. To me it sounded dogmatic and felt uncomfortable. Yes, regulations do make up for the absence of scientific conclusions about people and their reactions. But everyone is as unique as their circumstances. Generalizing about what's healthy and what isn't is destructive. I would rather think about people, myself included, one at a time before I conclude that they are either well or sick.

There are certain symptoms that are far more serious than others. Susan, an attractive thirty-nine-year-old patient, came to see me ten months after her husband died, complaining that she had lost all interest in things about which she had previously cared. These empty feelings began with her husband Matthew's suicide.

Susan told her story as if she were relating an event that had occurred to a stranger years ago. She described the circumstances of finding that her husband had shot himself with his shotgun. She said she had no feelings about the fact that he had killed himself, stating, "Dead is dead, what's the difference."

In future sessions she told me that for several months following the funeral it seemed to her that Matthew wasn't really dead. Her intellect acknowledged that he was, but somehow she *felt* that he was still alive. At seven-fifteen in the evening, the time Matt would usually arrive home from work, she would stand at the window watching for him to drive up into the garage. Rationally she knew he wouldn't be there, and yet she often bought his favorite foods, putting them at his place at the table. During this time she felt no sadness, only emptiness.

Susan was in emotional trouble. Her frozen affect and general disassociated reaction were my first cause for alarm:

she had slipped well beyond a mourning process. Left un-treated, she was likely to become increasingly out of touch with reality.

I was concerned with her denial of any feelings about the fact that her husband had taken his own life. Survivors of mates' suicides have long been thought by experts to be at greater risk for physical and mental health problems than widows and widowers who are bereaved from other causes of death. Very often denial, used the way Susan was using it, serves as an impenetrable wall against guilt. It took many sessions before her wall crumbled and Susan could talk about her stormy marriage, blaming herself for the marital conflicts and insisting that she was to blame for Matthew's suicide.

Susan's circumstances were not as unusual as many peo-ple would like to think. It is estimated that more than 27,000 people commit suicide in the United States each year and that men are three times more likely than women to die by their own action. The numbers are conservative because of the ambiguous circumstances of some deaths and society's need to deny suicide whenever possible. But whatever the numbers, suicide leaves in its wake widows with a complex set of feelings and social problems.

Another widow, Anna, was faced with her husband's family after her husband died from an overdose of sleeping pills. They created a "family myth" about her deceased hus-band, insisting he had died from a heart attack as a result of the extreme pressure at work. At first Anna resisted and tried to convince them of the truth, but then found it ex-tremely comforting to accept their reality. Thereafter she told everyone that he had died from a heart attack, totally avoiding her intense feelings that he willfully abandoned her. Anna, like Susan, slid into a make-believe world with make-believe feelings.

The term "pathological mourning" could be used about both Susan and Anna, but it seems unnecessary to use that designation. Labels are useful for therapists if they need them for paperwork such as agency reports or insurance claims. But for the most part labels are used by those who want to separate the "sick" from the "healthy." It's not that simple. What people see is not always a proper indication of what is really happening. The widow who carries on with her life in a seemingly productive way, without suffering the agony of grief, looks to many like someone who has finished the mourning process. Too often, however, the process may not even have started. Defenses used excessively, like Susan's and Anna's, can escalate into serious complications.

Intensity and duration of mourning are factors used by many clinicians to differentiate the normal from the pathological response. But the limits of these descriptions are very difficult to establish. How can anyone define *long, long enough,* and *too long*? What genius can determine that a year of mourning is healthy and a year and a half sick? Universal rules cannot work for us because we all experience both internal and external changes differently.

We widows wonder during our convalescence if we're actually functioning, if we're really okay. Much of the time we feel so strange that words like pathological, insane, and crazy lure and confuse us. Most widows aren't anywhere near pathological or crazy and for the few who are, there is help. Our "craziness" is neither a chronic state nor is it terminal.

My greatest concern in working with widows is to determine if they are stuck in their mourning process. Some-times, as with Susan and Anna, grief is arrested. I've worked with other widows who also carry on their lives as though nothing had happened. Some appear to be toned down, shut off; their entire response seems slight compared to the intensity of the relationship they describe. Others are stuck, always yearning and angry, and with a covert belief that their husbands will return some day. Extreme anger whose intensity doesn't abate also concerns me. Anger at the lost relationship is more like that of an abandoned child toward a deceased parent, which, in the early phases of mourning, appears transient and eventually passes. But when it doesn't, the anger goes on and on, eventually dis-rupting a whole existence, destroying one's professional life as well as personal relationships.

I look at what I've written and realize (again) how many of these symptoms I had, and how little by little their in-tensity dimmed. I briefly denied Leonard's death, then pre-tended I was fine, knowing full well I was not. Feeling out of control and stupid, I carried on periodic conversations with Leonard, sometimes asking advice or reporting an event I thought he'd appreciate. And I was angry, and scared!

My anchor and support had deserted me and, like a child, I raged at the world; sometimes in my darkest moments I felt as if my very survival were at risk. I even berated Leon-ard for having given me so much, arguing that it made my loss all the greater. My symptoms came and went as my life progressed—sometimes more intensely, sometimes less. They changed as I changed, not in a straight line or in an organized, labeled, scientific manner, but in the chaotic, unpredictable, unscientific process called mourning and called growth.

My expectation that the end of the first year would bring about major changes was based on a formula. I had to learn to accept other people's axioms only when they applied to me and not use them to support my notion of craziness when they didn't fit. If you are like me, you wish there were a universal law for feelings, but there isn't.

Non–Vital Statistics

We widows have our own language. We ask one another, "How's it going? How are you feeling?" and we answer, "Fine, a bit better . . . you know how it is." Translated: We got through another day and night, our health is about the same as it was yesterday, nothing catastrophic has happened during the last twenty-four hours—and although we continue to fall into an abyss, from time to time we do seem to be making progress in the job of gluing ourselves back together again.

We translate the degree of our misery: "fine" means "okay," "fair" means "sad," and "not so good" means "I'm in real trouble." We share our greatest fears either overtly or covertly with those who identify with us. Often we start a sentence and stop, knowing our widowed pals can finish it for us. Our angst is now allowed to surface only with one another; we've learned from other friends that certain behavior is no longer acceptable.

It's wonderful to be understood—to feel you can be yourself and show your *real* feelings. Living among the walking wounded who share your experience provides support and nurturing that make you feel protected. Unfortunately, like everything else in life, there's a negative side to this protection: We're at risk of becoming an island of loss, cut off from life's mainstream. While our goal is to reinforce one another in positive ways, we need to be vigilant about not reinforcing our negative selves. As loss calls these negative selves into being, we begin to feel contemptuous of others as well as of ourselves.

Often we sound like small children who blame themselves when faced with the loss of a parent, saying, "If I'd been a better little girl Mommy wouldn't have gone away," or, "If I'd done my homework Daddy wouldn't have gotten mad and left us." Now, as adults, we tend to blame ourselves because we're "bad" or because we've "failed." Our contempt for ourselves has taken the place of our early blame stage, immediately after our loss. "I was a bad wife" has turned into "I'm a bad person—I should have known earlier that my husband was sick." This sense of worthlessness now escalates into "I'm a disgusting failure: everything about me is recycled garbage." Our negative self-image germinates into flowering contempt; we look to other widows one more time to reinforce these feelings. Sybil, in my group, constantly demeaned herself and the rest of us by describing all widows as "bulging middles" and "middle-aged." Sybil weighed about a hundred and ten pounds, but her contempt for herself dictated her false description. In her effort to bond with us, to solidify our relationship, she didn't notice the negative impact she was having on our collective egos.

Another version of similar dynamics came from a seventy-nine-year-old relative who said to me after Leonard's death, "Pick your friends carefully, my dear. *My* only friends are young, divorced, or single women. I wouldn't be caught dead palling around with a bunch of boring old depressed widows." Confronted, she defended her position as being caring, loving, and helpful, when in fact it was a blatant put-down of herself; she had all the characteristics at which she sneered. Because she thought of *herself* as boring and depressed, she could only feel worthwhile through the eyes of her younger, more attractive friends.

One of the women in my widow group declared, "Widows should only be friends with their own kind—water seeks its own level." She failed to add that the "level" could get pretty low and that we were in danger of narrowing our perspectives.

My own version of contemptuous thinking was a conglomerate. Focusing on every negative aspect of my widowhood, I quoted studies and statistics that supported my position. Before, professionally, I had always meticulously studied data before using the information with patients because of my doubts and questions about accuracy and usefulness. Now, with all my widowed friends, I found myself extracting a sentence or two from unconfirmed research. "Did you know that one out of five widows will be dead within a year after her husband's funeral?" I would ask sagely. "And," I would go on, "most professional women leave their jobs within six months after their mates die because they lose interest in every aspect of life. Widows are more prone to accidents than any other group of people. Seventy percent of widows are financially bankrupt two years after their spouses' deaths."

As I shared these statistical gems I was aware that I was unable to talk about my increasing awareness that I was feeling better. I still had my black days, but generally, as the turning points occurred, I had begun to wonder what the next phase would be. I halfheartedly tried to shift the discussion from mourning, but then felt embarrassed. The message I was getting from the group was that there was no next phase; our present phase was the only and forever one. We clearly were wonderful for one another through the grieving process. It was the living process that lacked support.

At one group meeting Betsy brought in statistics on widows living in the United States. She wanted to start a movement that would include the twelve million widows reported in her census. It would be an adjunct to the women's liberation movement and would be called "Rights for the Angry and the Betrayed," or RAB.

Every group event was experienced differently since the members were all in emotionally different places. We had entered the group with our own histories, and each of us had been living her own unique existence since then. We had grown separately and together. Betsy was now actively moving outside our group to work with widows all over the United States.

Three group members reacted by trying to get Betsy to behave like her old, crippled, passive self; the other three expressed irritation with the concept of universal widowhood. I, feeling furious, fell in with the second group. Was I part of Betsy's census—a statistic? "God," I finally exploded, "How can people be *people* if they're simply statistics? Why are we now labeled 'angry and betrayed' by one of our own when we've spent months railing against being labeled by nonwidows?"

Betsy and her coterie became more militant. We widows, they said, had to stick together if we were to survive. We were not to engage in any social life with couples; we were united! Having been excluded, it was now our turn to exclude.

I suggested that these women sounded like the blacks and Puerto Ricans, fighting first with the establishment and then with one another. I asked Betsy when she and her followers would begin to fight with one another and once again split into smaller and more warlike factions?

The discussion reverted to more contempt: no one would want us; we weren't socially acceptable. We should see the writing on the wall and save face by turning away. The group was turning on itself.

The next group session began on a quieter note, but the issue of people versus statistics came up once again. Viewing myself as a statistic diminished me and added to my negative feelings of self-worth; seeing anyone as a statistic takes away from their uniqueness and their power. The group was still divided but, as always, ready to consider differences. Betsy returned with additional information to support her previous position that since we were being forced into a minority position, we would do well to organize and fight for recognition. Now she brought us statistics of widowers: two million, compared to twelve million widows. She flipped through the index cards she took from her purse. How, she challenged, would I suggest we return to the mainstream, given the statistics? A pall settled over the group as we awaited an answer. Betsy was talking about returning to the mainstream through remarriage. It was a staggering concept. Remarriage had never been mentioned before: we had mulled and chewed our way through hundreds of other words and issues but this one had never surfaced. Now everyone was looking at the floor, the ceiling, anyplace that guaranteed not looking at one another. Betsy's eyes were fixed on her index cards.

Pat broke the silence by suggesting that we wait till the next session to explore this major issue since the time for this session was almost over. Nobody moved. Sybil began to cry, saying she wasn't coming next week because even talking about replacing Tony would be too painful.

Despite Pat's suggestion, the group decided to continue. Aware that Betsy had brought up the problem of returning to the mainstream, I began to speak. I still refused to be a statistic; I wanted to be me. I was fully prepared to return to the mainstream as me, unique, individual, and alone. I hadn't the slightest interest in being part of a couple, but planned to live a complete and useful life. I tried to tell the group that we had moved to a different phase and could look toward a future. But considering remarriage was ridiculous. Everyone applauded but Betsy, who was angry with me for not joining her militant "Angry and Betrayed" group. Pat called a halt and we quietly and separately left the session.

I returned the following week determined to restate my position, about which I had obsessed relentlessly since the last meeting. To my chagrin and later humiliation I delivered a monologue that went something like this:

I will never remarry; there is absolutely no need to do so. I loved being married to Leonard and the thought of remarriage is distasteful. My view is that what you've done once successfully can't be redone. Stop while you're ahead; you're only lucky once and at best marriage is a chancy crap shoot. Besides, why should I remarry? I have finally managed to prove I can take care of myself. I didn't want to have to prove it, but now that I have, I'm not going to quit. I don't need anyone; I don't have to depend on anyone for anything; I'm my own person. I could have happily lived forever with Leonard, but not having had that choice, I've put together a life that works. Stronger and more capable than ever, I can handle anything that comes my way. I've been forced to use parts of myself I never knew existed, all related to competence, which can only be used in my

single existence. I have overdepended on people—
including Leonard—in my past but I'll never do it again.
I would like a man in my life, but one who comes and
goes and gives me my independence to also come and
go. A companion with whom to go to the theater, movies, and concerts—and with whom I have dinner and
generally have fun. In other words, I want a female
friend who's male. I've always enjoyed men and would
like to have one or two among my new circle of friends.
My main priority is to continue along the path I've been
on since Leonard's death. I am determined to remain
functional as a separate entity and to be more than I am
now—smarter, wiser, more integrated. I feel I can do
that only if I remain true to my disconnected, unattached identity.

When I stopped talking, Betsy smiled at me for the first
time in weeks.

Thinking the Unthinkable

Betsy's mention of remarriage caused a major shift within
the group. It was as if we'd been given permission to explore a brand-new subject with the potential of interrupting
everything that was now comfortably familiar. Dealing with
loss framed our days; like chronic illness, our mourning left
little room for expectations of change. We had, of course,
been able to discuss certain modifications. We talked about
challenges in the world of work, and we had endlessly compared our social relationships of the past to our current
ones. We had examined the impact of our spouses' deaths
on our families, our financial situations, our living arrange-

ments, and our daily choices. Symbolically, each of us carried reinforcement and encouragement from past relationships. We had totally mastered the commandments and regulations of our unattached existences.

Now Betsy, the person least interested in men, was forcing us to address a new subject. How ironic! In her quest for support of her anti-man position, she had managed to open up the terrifying consideration that marriage was, although statistically unlikely, a possibility for the women in our group. Suddenly it became an option with which we might have to deal. It felt as if we were having to look at our feelings without the framework of the past. After all, "How can a widow think about *re*marriage?" Sybil wondered aloud. "The past is the present and we're all still very much married."

The two men in the group had different views. Norman was sure that he could easily have a future with a new wife—if she were willing to move into his present home. He explained that he could never move away from his beautiful suburban house in Montclair, New Jersey, because his late wife had furnished it so beautifully and so lovingly. All their possessions and dreams were in that house. "So, of course," Norman said, "no woman could expect me to leave and move somewhere else."

Cliff was concerned with his daughter's response if she knew he could even consider a new wife. After all, she had had a screaming tantrum the first time he went out with someone new. Despite her subsequent reluctant acceptance of his increased social life, Cliff wasn't sure she could handle his remarrying, which he actually had been quietly contemplating.

We women eyed the two men suspiciously. Despite my monologue the previous week, I was feeling envious of the men's clear and straight statements that they wanted new mates. Cliff said that although he had no one in mind, he was sure that once he felt it appropriate for him to marry, it wouldn't take him long to make his move.

Vera, enraged, called Cliff and Norman heartless beasts who thought one woman was the same as another—that they could marry at the drop of a hat without any loyalty to their past attachments.

Betsy, quoting the women's liberation motto, said, "Women mourn, men replace." When the other women applauded, the men totally withdrew from the discussion.

I withdrew too, thinking about the days when Leonard was first diagnosed with a terminal form of leukemia. I recalled lying on my bed in those early days and wondering if I would remarry, then dismissing it as an option. Later, Leonard had been very direct about his feeling: "You will remarry," he said. "I wouldn't want it any other way." He went on at length about what my life would be like if I lived alone and gave his reasons for my remarrying. I was furious with him for even mentioning the word: it underscored the certainty of his death and minimized the value of our relationship.

Leonard defended himself against my fury by begging me to accept the finality of his illness, pointing out that his wanting me to remarry was an affirmation of our own marriage. If a person has been happy in a marriage, he suggested, she will want to repeat the experience. But I couldn't listen, and slammed the door to his hospital room as I stormed out.

It got worse. One evening, while talking to a handsome doctor who had come by to check his condition, Leonard sweetly inquired about the doctor's marital status. He said he was single and after he left the room Leonard told me to "remember him for afterwards." I picked up the plastic water pitcher and tossed it at him. We were both appalled by my uncontrolled temper, then burst out laughing as I cleaned up the mess. He had meant well, but I was unable to deal with the thought of being married to anyone else. My pain was so intense that I couldn't accept or comprehend his generosity and loving concern for me. Now, two years later, my eyes filled with tears as I recalled his kindness to me and his tolerance of my ingratitude.

Sybil asked me why the tears—after all, she pointed out, you're so clear about the future. Referring to my monologue of the previous week she said she was less clear about living alone forever and didn't share my enthusiasm. Locked in my sadness, I had no answer for her.

The group now split into two factions—Vera, Betsy, and I championing the single status against Sybil and the two men. Despite the split, we were all struggling with monumentally important issues. Everything connected to a new life would have to be examined, but right now we focused on remarriage itself.

I had already addressed the subject of remarriage with Rita, a patient. She had been referred to me by her internist, who recommended a psychiatric consultation because of a six-month history of panic attacks. Rita experienced extreme fear accompanied by sweating, shortness of breath, palpitations, and chest pains. Her internist was satisfied with the results of a complete physical, which included an EKG, a glucose tolerance test, and other blood studies. He was convinced her symptoms were emotionally caused and referred her to me.

Five minutes into our first session, Rita told me she was afraid she was dying. Recently remarried, she and her husband, a widower of two years, had decided to destroy all their possessions from their previous lives. They wanted to "begin again," and had systematically sold, given away, or auctioned off their belongings. Everything from pots and pans to furniture was newly purchased by them jointly. She had no children from her previous marriage and his only son had been living in Germany for twenty years. They saw themselves as unencumbered and free of their past lives, having to deal only with the shared present.

Rita's acute anxiety reaction had begun eight weeks after her marriage to Michael, when he took her to meet his oldest friend, Dan. Also a widower, Dan was living in the house he had shared with his late wife, surrounded by her photographs and filled with other mementos of their life together. Dan had questioned Rita about her first husband, and it was after they left him that Rita began to experience intense panic symptoms—sweaty hands, fuzzy vision, numb arms. Terrified, she thought she would be dead by morning. Her symptoms continued through the following day, but then abruptly disappeared. Trying to figure out what had caused them, Rita put it down to Dan's questions. She couldn't understand why he would have cared about her past. What was he insinuating? Was he trying to cause trouble in her new marriage?

In the following weeks her anxiety attacks returned and escalated, as did her ruminations about Dan. By the time she came to see me, she was in an acute crisis. I suggested we meet three times a week, first to relieve her of her debilitating symptoms, and then to explore their cause. Rita readily agreed and immediately began to work at therapy as if it were her lifeline. She opened doors to her previously closed unconscious and rushed along, shedding physical problems one by one along the way.

Her symptoms were relatively easy to heal; the actual

roots that they masked were another matter. Rita discovered she had short-circuited her feelings by moving into a new marriage without allowing herself to go through the process of mourning. She had found in Michael a willing collaborator who supported her need to jump over the process instead of going through it; he had his own needs, which were being met by hers. Together they had agreed to move into the future without including their pasts. Now she was having a reaction, symptomatized by anxiety attacks.

Rita recognized almost immediately that she had to begin at the beginning. She had been married fifteen years when her husband was first diagnosed with a rare form of bone cancer. The doctor's prognosis that he would die quickly and painlessly was wrong on both counts. The terminal illness lasted five years. Rita spoke of her feelings of being trapped inside her own body as she watched him deteriorate; her increasing feelings of helplessness turned into rage as the years passed. Rita became her husband's legs and eventually his eyes and ears as she nursed him through the years. They had made few friends before the onset of the illness and as it progressed Rita became completely isolated. By the time her husband died she was in profound psychological trouble. She confided in no one, put her home on the market, and moved immediately to an apartment in a nearby city. She decided to finish her college education, halted twenty-seven years earlier, and returned to school. It was there that she met Michael, a professor at the university. Attracted to each other, they quickly threw themselves into a whirlwind romance, each barely mentioning their former lives and neither one asking any questions. Michael, because of a painfully unsuccessful former marriage, happily accepted the unspoken pact of silence. Both were satisfied to live in the here and now, not knowing they were encapsulated in a bubble of denial.

The bubble burst with the advent of Rita's symptoms. Michael and Rita began to fight; Rita unfavorably comparing Michael to her former husband, Michael suddenly realizing that Rita reminded him of his former wife. Both were taking second looks at each other and at their marriage.

Rita brought Michael to several sessions with me in an attempt to recapture their early feelings, but neither she nor Michael could fix the unfixable. They reluctantly agreed that they had nothing to keep them together and their marriage officially ended the following year.

Knowing that Rita and Michael were an extreme and dramatic example of an impulsive marriage didn't keep me from seeing them as living examples of what could happen to anyone in our bereavement group. Once again I realized how wounded we all were and that under the best of circumstances major transitions are a gamble. Once we managed them with relative ease—marriage, having children, changing jobs—but now everything had changed. Desperation, loneliness, and panic could, as they had with Rita and Michael, cloud our perceptions. We were candidates for making a major mistake, all of us potential victims on the brink of disaster.

I asked Cliff and Norman how they were able to be so positive about remarriage in the near future. Cliff said he and Norman were far better equipped to consider it because they had been dating women for months. "When are you all going to shape up and get moving?" he inquired. Norman jumped aboard: "It's about time. How the hell can we talk about remarriage before we talk about dating?" He looked around the room. His eyes locked with mine. "You," he said, "better get cracking. You'd better switch gears.

You're stuck in neutral." Once more Norman was on my case. I shot back, "At least I'm out of reverse. Be grateful for little things." Everyone laughed except Betsy, who was still flipping through index cards.

The air-conditioning wasn't working in the room so we stopped the group early. Bless the air-conditioning! My anxiety was overworking: the word "dating" had made my skin crawl. No one over thirty-five should seriously use that word; the concept was laughable. What did people of our vintage use to express going out? I wondered. Listen, I told myself sternly, Cliff and Norman use the word and they're the same vintage you are.

Unbelievable! I thought I'd find it much easier to jump over dating (if that was what I was supposed to call it) and go back to thinking about remarriage. But then I realized I wasn't able to think about it after all. I had gone back: immersed and enmeshed in my past. I found it impossible to picture a different life from the one I knew. Norman was right: I was stuck in neutral. How could I visualize a future without having the vaguest idea of what was to happen tomorrow or the next day?

7

Sorting Out Feelings and What to Do about Them

Men

My head felt as if it were in a blender—thoughts whirring so chaotically I couldn't think about what to think about. "Start dating," Norman had said. For a moment I visualized an elegant restaurant, candlelit, filled with well-dressed people. I was with a faceless man; the two of us were locked in intense conversation. I froze—this idea could lead to one dangerous thought after another.

I needed the chaos contained. I phoned Betsy, knowing she specialized in focusing on singular issues with clear, sharp edges. Unlike me, she never saw two sides of the same coin or considered different interpretations of a problem. She was of the yes/no school, which sometimes annoyed me but now seemed to offer a remedy to my increasing anxiety.

I began by asking for a reaction to the last group meeting. Most of the material had bored her to tears and seemed like a rerun. I was astonished: how could she be bored with weighty material that was loaded with explosive possibilities? Citing previous sessions, she pointed out that we'd already talked about social lives, friendships, new and old connections to the point where she was ready to scream. I returned to Norman's suggestion that I start dating. Betsy replied straightforwardly, "If it bothers you, don't do it."

I envied Betsy's complacency. Her commitment to rights for widows left her no time to worry about the things I now found myself chewing over. I was surprised at the impact Norman's attack had had on me. We'd been dueling since our first meeting, so why was I suddenly coming unglued?

My therapist had told me years before that when I felt unglued there was guilt underneath the feeling and I should try to figure out what the guilt was about. I looked into the mirror: "You guilty?" I asked innocently. "About what?" I visualized Leonard's face, trying to put a dark frown of disapproval on it. But all I managed to see was his loving smile. Honesty forced me to give it up; the source of my guilt was coming from somewhere totally unrelated to Leonard.

I had a secret that only one other person knew. I had managed to conceal it from my group and everyone else then in my life. Three months after Leonard's death, when I was in the pit of despair and overwhelmed by feelings that nothing could ever be the same again, I received a phone call from an old flame. Having read Leonard's obituary in a back issue of *Time*, he called to offer his condolences. We talked briefly and stiltedly. The following week he was coming to New York, so we set a time to meet—two old friends who hadn't seen each other for over twenty years would have a drink and catch up on each other's lives.

I thought about our meeting continuously. What did he look like now? He had been compellingly attractive. Speaking of looks, what about me? Staring into the mirror I decided that I looked like an older me. I moved on to other considerations. Was he still an architect? More important, was he still married? The "what-ifs" and the "buts" proliferated as my capacity to deal with reality evaporated.

I confided in a close friend, who was ecstatically seduced by the romantic nature of the reunion. "All those years have gone by and he still thinks of you? Wow!" We were both impressed. She and I staged the evening—how I should dress, how I should present myself, my mood, even my choice of subjects for conversation. We discussed every aspect of the meeting except how I might feel. It was as if I were acting a part in a play; my feelings, of course, were not an issue. I jumped from one unfinished fantasy to another: what if he . . . could he be . . . might he rescue me . . . Suddenly there was the possibility of a possibility.

Finally the night arrived. It began with friends catching up on old times and ended with lovers working on unfinished business. He was still married and sad; I was sad, lonely, and terrified. The combination provided us with an excuse to resume our relationship.

I know other widows who've had similar experiences—old relationships reinstated either by them or by their former loves. Pamela, a widowed friend, told me that during the six months her husband Ed was terminally ill she fantasized repeatedly about Gerry, a former boyfriend whom she had stopped seeing when she met her husband. Despite her strong attachment to Ed, Pamela called

Gerry two weeks after her husband's funeral. They picked up exactly where they had left off years before. Six months later, looking back at her actions, she realized she had done it to prove to herself that she was still alive. "I felt so dead I had to know that Ed hadn't taken me with him."

Ann, another widow, talked about how she had agreed to have an affair with an old love, now married to a friend, because she didn't have to worry about his reaction to her aging body. His image of her from the past made change a nonissue. "It was kind of like with Dan [her late husband]—he always saw me the way I was when we first met."

A patient of mine phoned her ex-lover when she heard from a mutual friend that his wife was terminally ill. She offered him her understanding of and identification with his trauma. They began seeing each other immediately, despite the fact that his wife was still alive. After the wife's death, my patient never saw the lover again. He was on to other relationships that did not remind him of his wife's death.

What we four women had in common was relief at suddenly having someone in our lives with whom we had an established relationship. The work had been done years ago; here were men who knew and understood us. They loved us once and could love us again. How comfortable and safe it all felt! My lover had come back offering me strength and support. How reminiscent of a past life that seemed so much easier! Twenty years before, life seemed filled with possibilities, challenges, and hope. Now my life was filled by loneliness, emptiness, hopelessness. My lover offered me romantic nurturing. He made me feel alive and attractive, far removed from death and aloneness. I needed a loving friend, so when he offered to be one, I gratefully accepted. Then I tried to make it more. I forgot that past loves are *past* for a reason; I had married someone else for that reason. My lover was married and metabolically out of sync with me. Neither fact had changed. Our relationship hadn't worked twenty-one years before and couldn't work now.

My lover from the past was a symptom of my wish to move backward; moving forward terrified me. My unconscious was hoping that life would repeat itself—chronologically my lover had come first, followed by Leonard. Perhaps, therefore, everything would be the same again.

Of course it wasn't. After our initial meeting, we saw each other several times. But for me each contact increasingly emphasized the difference between our present and past beings. Initially I relished playing the part of my young self: I slipped gracefully into past behavior as he related accordingly. But when I became uncomfortable acting like a child, my lover had great difficulty with the grown-up me. Also, after an initial and perfunctory inquiry about Leonard, he acted as if Leonard had been a minor part of life, dealing with me as the young, undeveloped single girl of another era. We found increasingly less to talk about as our interest waned. Soon we parted, as friends who would remain forever out of touch with each other. I felt silly, guilty, and thankful. I was embarrassed by my fantasies but grateful for having moved emotionally to a new place. My guilt about married men had been a huge issue in our initial relationship and now it intensified, which produced a renewed sense of worthlessness. I vowed never to tell anyone. Only my best friend knew and that was bad enough. Some day I would have to deal with it, but I would postpone it until I was ready.

Ready or not, Norman was forcing me to think about it *now* by confronting me about dating. Then Nancy, a recently widowed colleague, told me about her first move back to a world with men in it. Her children, without telling her, placed an ad in *New York* magazine's personals section for singles. It read: "Attractive sixty-year-old professional widowed female hopes to meet equally attractive, available, sympathetic, fun-loving male with whom she can play. She is not interested in a serious relationship; she is hoping for ease, warmth, and laughter. P.O. Box 208."

Nancy's children clipped the printed version out of the magazine and attached a note saying: "You wouldn't do this yourself, so we are doing it for you. Please come back to the world of the living. We miss you . . . Happy birthday!"

Nancy's first reaction was horror, then laughter, followed by curious interest that turned to fear on seeing her ad surrounded by ads for people in their twenties and thirties. She mused about the chances of anyone's answering, then worried that they might. She was astounded when the first of several responses arrived. Her children were delighted that their plan was working. They literally dressed her for her date, picking her clothes and changing her makeup. They turned the event into a game, supporting her through her first date in thirty-nine years. Instead of returning to their own homes, they awaited her return upstairs in her house. At midnight she arrived, victorious. She had conquered her fears and survived.

Lucky Nancy—it was behind her now. I still had to take my first plunge into icy waters. Even as I told myself the idea revolted me, I knew I was lying. In truth I missed being with men and would have to find a way to relearn the ways of doing it. Norman was right.

Where Are They?

Norman and Cliff had it easy. They were invited to fill in at dinner parties by every couple they knew and they were introduced to all of their friends' unattached females. Their male friends shared their bounty, passing along phone numbers. Norman met a woman who, after their relationship turned out to be unsatisfactory, casually introduced him to four of her widowed friends. Cliff got numerous phone calls from women he'd never met who had heard he was a recent widower.

The two brought their dating tales to the group. Obsessed with women, they boasted their way through one entire meeting. Going out every night, they had now reached the point where they were both exhausted and broke. But they went on acting like children let loose in a candy store. Betsy, Sybil, and I showed our disgust by attempting to change the subject, but then Vera asked Norman to introduce her to a man, which caused a major disaster. Norman presented her with Carl, a lawyer who immediately became enamored of her. He called Norman the next day, thanking him profusely and declaring, "I've lost my heart to that beauty."

On their third date, Vera suggested they attend Sunday services together. Carl, distraught, called Norman to check on Vera's religion. Norman answered that it had been weeks since religion had come up in the group and that he had no idea who was Jewish, Catholic, or Protestant, nor did he care. Carl was in a frenzy: religion was the highest priority on his list. On his next date with Vera he informed her that he had to stop seeing her because he was an Orthodox Jew, so it just couldn't work. Vera, immensely attracted to Carl, was desolate. She told him that although she was a Catholic she had been happily married to a Protestant for fifteen years, proving religion wasn't that important. Carl, adamant, disagreed and said good-bye, which left Vera in tears for several days.

Sybil and I were infuriated with Norman for his total lack of consideration. Vera's experience only reinforced our own anxieties about potential ambushes awaiting us. Betsy's predictable reaction was that men could never be trusted, so why the fuss?

Sybil met *her* first date on a jet going to Oregon to visit her children. She was sitting next to him, talking her way across the country, when he suddenly asked her to have dinner with him the next night. Having had no contact with men since her husband's death, she surprised herself by accepting his invitation. "Good God," she said later, "my mother would have died all over again! She told me never to go out with a man unless I knew his pedigree. I could have been strangled and left in an alley like women you read about."

But Sybil returned to tell the group that she had not only survived the dinner date but was planning to see the man on her next trip to visit her children. "I guess forty years later things are different, very different," she said. But we all knew she was still worried about what her mother would have said.

My stepson-in-law introduced me to my first date after Leonard's death (my recycled love affair didn't count) by having him phone for an engagement. I dreaded it; I hadn't had to make female-to-male conversation with a stranger in over twenty years. What in the world do two people of the opposite sex who don't know each other talk about? "Self," I said, "why is it so hard? I've been talking with ease to people of both sexes for years. Why is this so different?"

Actually, the last thing I wanted to do was persuade a strange man that I was appealing and attractive. Young girls play that game, but just thinking about it made me sick. Was I, in fact, still attractive? I had gotten much better about mirroring myself, but unfortunately I had been listening to Norman and Cliff, two self-anointed critics, two bozos of beauty, discuss their dates—one was too fat; another had piano legs; a third, a pretty redhead, had pasty skin. When their dates had been physically acceptable, Norman or Cliff would whimper "smart," "dumb," "weak," "competitive."

I postponed my date with Peter for an extra week. My son-in-law crossly informed me that I was taking a big risk, that the man might meet someone else in the meantime. I didn't tell him that would have been fine with me.

However, Peter and I did meet the following week in a quaint Italian restaurant near my office. He was tall, athletically built, and good-looking. Divorced, he had a fourteen-year-old son to whom he was charmingly devoted. Much of our conversation focused on his son's concern about finding a girl to take to the junior prom. We also talked about our work—Peter worked long, strenuous hours as a money manager. Asking me in turn about my patients, he showed considerable knowledge about the complexities of clinical situations.

I felt unexpectedly comfortable. I wasn't even displeased by his inquiries about Leonard, nor his summation of the events that caused his divorce. Having finished a pleasant dinner, we were waiting for the check when he casually said, "Knowing your stepchildren's ages doesn't tell me your age." He waited as I wondered whether to tell the truth. Still unsure, I asked even more casually than he, "How old are you?" "Fifty," he said, "and you?" A year younger than he was, I was delighted to tell the truth. Snapping his credit card on the table, Peter stamped his foot and said with disappointment, "It won't work, damn it. I have to have someone thirty-nine or younger."

Stunned, I sat there saying nothing, which I have regretted ever since. I wish I'd said, "I know what you mean—I was hoping for the same thing."

Of course, I wasn't. But it would have helped me deal with my hurt and rage at him. Instead, saying nothing about his intolerable conceit, I meekly let him take me home, shake my hand, and say good night. I was in a state. Confused, humiliated, and scared, I felt like rubbish, trashed simply because of age. Where is it written that, younger than he, I was too old for him? A distorted equation seemed to have made it so. To paraphrase the writer Virgilia Peterson, women see gray hair on a man and lovingly recall their fathers; men see gray hair on a woman and run like hell.

Men can go out with younger women, if they choose to, and most choose to, leaving women their age and older totally ignored. And so the already small number of available men shrinks dramatically as women grow older. Given the facts, it's amazing how many widows of all ages have men in their lives. My widowed father fell madly in love with a widow two years older than he. They had a grand, romantic relationship for over six years, then he died. They traveled together, ate every meal together, were always on the phone to each other—all without thinking about age. He characterized her as a delicious human being with whom he could live out his life, and she described him as the most exciting man she'd ever known.

A seventy-four-year-old colleague, whom I call the merry marrying widow, is currently married to her fifth husband, a prosperous judge who calls his bride "my magical dream." In between husbands four and five, my colleague informed me that she couldn't survive unmarried and couldn't imagine living alone. She told me she would find someone. Despite her past history, I thought her chances were nil. I was wrong.

How do women meet men? And why do some women never meet anyone? Often it's by choice. My traveling companion to China had decided early in the game to live alone. She has a satisfying life and feels her decision was the right one, as do many women who, after healthy, thoughtful consideration choose to live without a man.

What about women who want to meet men but are unable to? They often explain it by the scarcity and the age differential. A sixty-three-year-old patient told me, "Big joke . . . I met a man at a dinner party who was attractive but decided not to go out with him because he was seventy-three. I was afraid he'd get sick and I'd end up taking care of him. Then, last night, I saw him again, in a restaurant, with a woman much younger than me. She was having the time of her life! Do you think I was wrong, that the joke's on me?"

I don't think any of it is a joke. All of it involves serious decisions thoughtfully made by the individual. Generally speaking, the less rigid we are, the better our lives become. Flexibility helps. We're living in a different time and place from before we married, so it's very likely our expectations and demands will also be different. The same patient who turned down the seventy-three-year-old man was later to meet and enjoy a seventy-two-year-old, "a swinging, twice-widowed man who will probably outlive me with his damn health foods and the miraculous way he takes care of himself."

But what about the healthy, flexible, willing, attractive widows who don't meet men? That dilemma exists, but not to the extent that statistics (still my enemy) suggest. They exclude women who don't want men, and women living with men, or going out with men, playing with men, and those women looking who will eventually meet men.

Assuming you want a man in your life, you will have to present your best self, both physically and emotionally. How you feel about yourself will dictate the care you give yourself; both affect the Man Dilemma. Ellen, a friend of mine, gained forty pounds after her husband died. She let her hair became a straggly mess, wore ill-fitting clothes, skipped wearing makeup. Asked why, she said she didn't care, since Matt, her husband, could no longer see her. At the same time she griped about the dearth of available men, insisting that if she found one, he'd have to accept her "as is." Months later, after being on an intensive diet (her first step toward regaining her former physical self), she admitted she had been hiding her fear of being hurt again underneath her layer of fat.

Fear of pain also affects our presentation of our emotional selves. I looked okay but was socially impatient and intolerant, finding fault with everyone and everything. Looking back at myself, I see a judgmental, bitter woman inwardly raging at the world but outwardly criticizing and undermining others. Who, male or female, would want to spend time with such a cranky malcontent without a nice word to say? Many widows around me were doing better because they had a positive feeling about the future—they were the ones making it happen. Others, like me, focusing on the negative, were unknowingly making it *not* happen.

Sex

I got clear, sharply defined messages about sex from my parents: nice girls are virgins until their wedding night;

you're a nice girl, therefore you will be a virgin when you marry. I asked my mother how something so wrong a day before marriage could become all right one day later. A Victorian remnant, my mother dismissed my question and left me to figure it out.

I wasn't alone. Many of my peers in college were questioning old attitudes, experimenting with new concepts and behaviors. Night after night the dorm was pervaded by intense discussions for and against freer sexual expression. Unknowingly, we were the precursors of the sixties sexual revolution, and by the time it exploded we had converted our parents' views into our own. Then we had to watch as our children struggled with their freedom in much the same way as we had struggled with our lack of it.

We were as little help to them in sexual matters as our parents had been to us. Eventually we had all found a way that worked as long as we lived our sexual lives in the familiar framework that we helped to shape.

As a widow I found myself directly in the middle of foreign territory: another generation's principles, values, and beliefs. I was freed from my parents' punitive, binding views, but nowhere near liberated enough to accept the views of young, unattached men and women who dealt with sex in a routine manner, as an unspecial part of their lives—frequent, casual, one-night stands, without thought or passion. It was just there, something they did.

I talked to widows of different ages, finding the younger the widow, the less alienated she felt from the world of the unattached. Josephine, thirty-one, was ready, three months after being widowed, to begin going out with men. If having a sexual encounter was likely, she bravely discussed her loyalty to her late husband with her sister-in-law, who urged her to let go of the past. Encouraged by her approval, sex became part of Josephine's life again.

Vera, my young friend from the group, was far less anxious about sex than either Sybil or me. We tended to make a federal case of it. Vera was quiet about it most of the time, but when she did talk, she sounded as if she had accepted its inevitability.

Most older widows were appalled, like me, by the changed attitudes. One dealt with the chaos by going to the other extreme: she managed to make it a nonissue. Marie, married at twenty, expected, forty-three years later as a widow, to be "treated like a lady"—wined, dined, and courted before having sex with a man. She had gone to bed with her husband only after she married him and was determined to repeat that first experience.

Marie was frozen in a forgotten world. She repeatedly talked about her need for a relationship with a man, but didn't acknowledge the fact that the men she met were put off by her aloofness. Her behavior reminded me of my high school days when we played the "he can do—but he can't *ever* do" games. Marie, terrified, tried to resolve sexual issues by never letting sex become part of a relationship.

Leslie, a fifty-six-year-old patient, overreacted in the other direction. She totally embraced *all* the new freedoms, sleeping with every man who desired her. She even kept a file of her sexual partners' performances and preferences. Leslie's ego was being stroked and patted by these men, but she found little enjoyment in her sexual exploits. Her feeling that she was in a dark dungeon of emptiness remained unchanged. She was a little like Lenore, a young friend, who had been impressed with Erica Jong's book *Fear of Flying*. In it Jong coined the expression "zipless fuck," describing casual sexual intercourse as nonattaching, impersonal, isolated—a meaningless encounter. Lenore never worked through her sexual conflicts during her marriage and now, as a recent widow, chose the zipless fuck as her solution. Unhappy, lonely, and frustrated, she gave up her decision to play the liberated, fearless woman on the loose.

Diane, another widow, said that at her husband's funeral his business associate told her that she would soon need male companionship and comfort. He suggested that she would also want warmth and sex, and when she did, she should call him.

Furious, Diane told him that he had the taste of a pig and that he should stay away from her. But six months later she recalled what he had said. Although she wasn't all that interested in the sex part, she was interested in the warmth and comfort he had suggested. She called him and told him she was ready to accept his offer.

I wasn't clear about my own feelings. When I forced myself to explore them, I found a composite of Marie, Leslie, Lenore, and Diane. I longed for the safety of Marie's fairy tales, the ease of Leslie's flamboyant acting out, the objective, disinterested quality of Lenore's early enthusiasm for the "zipless fuck," and Diane's longing for warmth.

But even the most rudimentary aspects of sex felt overwhelming and terrifying. How would I take off my clothes? I wondered, as if contemplating a new pursuit. And what if by chance I managed to be without clothes . . . My mind froze. My body, never a tranquil friend, had nonetheless been a part of me. We'd had our fights—it wanted to be more corpulent than I wanted it to be; arbitrarily, I chose one weight, while my body, just as arbitrarily, chose a higher one. We had compromised successfully, until now.

Along with not liking me, I very much didn't like my body. Lenore, for whom it was clearly not an issue, told me to keep my clothes on and turn off the lights.

A wise colleague made a more constructive suggestion. "You are afraid to be seen by a new pair of eyes, but you're forgetting the other half of the equation: *your* eyes are looking at someone too."

I had been harshly demanding of myself to have the non-sagging perfect body, preferably of the age when I first married. It never occurred to me that men who might see my outlines could also have deficient bodies.

"How come," my colleague inquired, "you're so critical of *you?* Are you planning an affair with a movie star who is only interested in someone who's physically flawless?" Having no specific plans for movie stars or anyone else, I soon resolved not to sleep with anyone.

AIDS entered the picture. Almost every publication crossing my desk emphasized the physical risks associated with sex. Herpes, once the scourge of concern, had taken a backseat to AIDS. We in the health profession were now intensely concerned about AIDS in very much the same way that years ago we had focused on pregnancy and birth control.

During the day I worried about my patients as I listened to them talk about their sex lives and we discussed ways of protecting themselves from contracting AIDS. At night I worried about how it was affecting my own life. I was furious that someday it might become a personal issue too. How could life have conspired to put me in this position? It wasn't so long ago that I had commented to Leonard that one of the comforting things about longevity in marriage was not having to be concerned about AIDS.

Now I had a new equation: abstinence equals health. It

didn't feel like a major deprivation since sexual intercourse was not a high priority of mine. I yearned instead for physical closeness—holding, touching, warmth. I wanted cuddling, a hug before sleep, a secret shared late at night while the rest of the world slept. I knew I couldn't get AIDS from these things, but could I have these things without having sex?

I checked with my friends. Linda, to validate her attractiveness, wanted a lot of sex with different men. She was convinced that the safest candidates were married men, safe from a health standpoint and also safe "because they'll never ask me to give up my new, free life-style."

Selma, another friend, had a heated discussion with her gynecologist when he told her she was too old at sixty-seven to be interested in sex. It was time, he said, for her to sublimate her sexual energies by taking up a new hobby. I had known Selma's gynecologist professionally for many years. He was a bitter man, the product of a broken family whose mother had made sexual advances to his friends during his adolescence. Antiwoman to start with, he had chosen a profession in which he could act out his sadistic feelings. Like many people, he felt painfully uncomfortable with the sexual side of the middle-aged and elderly.

Sylvia was married at eighteen and widowed at forty-five. She "went looking for the kinky," checking out sex clubs and taking part in orgies. She equated her zest for sex with overeating or excessive drinking, attempting to convince her friends that kinky sex was just a lark. Fear stopped her in her tracks. She witnessed a sexual encounter in which another woman was physically abused. Terrified, she retreated from her dangerous pursuit. Knowing she needed help, she joined a widows' group in which she hoped she would be able to explore the reasons for her sexual choices.

My patient Catherine needed help dealing with her teen-age children about a man she had met two years after her husband's death. Her children, angry and resentful when she started going out with men, had slowly come around to accepting it. Catherine and her new friend, now facing a powerful sexual attraction for each other, couldn't find a way to act on it. Catherine realized that her children would erupt with negative reactions if they thought she was sex-ually involved. A male friend was okay, but sex was unac-ceptable. Their dad had been the only man who could enter Mommy's bed, and now that he was dead she should sleep alone.

After several months and much thought, Catherine fi-nally announced to her children that she was going away for a weekend with some friends. Her children accepted her statement without further questioning because either they actually believed it, or they wanted to believe it.

Catherine's children's loyalty to their father was very much like mine to Leonard. "Till death do us part" was translated into "till I die." However, I knew that Leonard would have found such a sexual commitment unwarranted and unhealthy. He would have challenged my obsession with AIDS and other sexually communicable diseases, ac-knowledging their existence while at the same time suggest-ing that I was using them as a smokescreen. "How do you plan to live the rest of your life," he would have said, "with-out the closeness that's a part of sex? You'd better believe that life is for the living and that sex is part of life."

This mental conversation helped me bring up the subject of sex in my group. I already knew more about Cliff's and Norman's sex lives than I wished to know. But I was curious about Vera and Sybil. (Betsy had already let us know she wasn't remotely interested in sex.) Vera confided that, having met a kind, considerate, and understanding man, she had decided one night to "shut my eyes, hold my nose, peel off my clothes and do it—just to get it over with." We all laughed, recognizing the sentiment.

I stopped laughing when I discovered that prim and proper Sybil had also "gotten it over with." While visiting her children in Oregon, she also saw the man she had met on the plane. She spoke earnestly of her amazement that a man in his mid-seventies could be so sexually active. She was outraged that people classified older men as either impotent or dirty old men.

Norman and Cliff seemed strangely threatened by Sybil's experience and observations. Norman handled his anxiety by attacking me. "You brought up the subject this week, my dear, and you're the quietest person in the room."

I had a sudden urge to tell him I was about to have a sex-change operation, or was contemplating opening a whorehouse for men like him. Once more, Norman was compelling me to do more work on myself. It was time to probe and examine my feelings honestly so that someday soon they would be understood and resolved.

Space

One of my biggest problems was with space. The idea of anyone else being in my space made me panic. Concealing my fears under a ton of rationalization—my apartment was too small, it couldn't accommodate company, there was no dining room—I maintained strict control over my home, unable to imagine sharing my space even for one night. I told friends about the advantages of living alone, completely negating the twenty years of pleasure I had living with Leonard. I reveled in the nonsharing aspects of my new life. My most frequently used words became "I," "mine," and "space."

I was aware of the vast change in my outlook, explaining that it was symptomatic of my growth. I could not only *live* alone, I could *choose* to live alone.

To me, empty space represented independence and maturity. What it also represented was profound loneliness, which I denied. Although I was no longer unhappy in the sharp, painful way I had been at first, now I was surrounded by a wall of quiet depression that protected me from all intruders.

Some of my unmarried feminist friends supported me. So did many married friends, who reinforced my declaration of independence by their contention that I was in a better position than they were! Further strengthening came from the examples of space-sharing that I witnessed around me.

Three months after her husband died, Francine invited a male friend to move into her apartment. Later she found herself enraged with him for never putting the toilet seat down and applauded my position of excluding all men from my space.

Jackie, another friend, also regretted her hasty decision to share her home. In a panic after the death of her husband, she advertised for a student, offering room and board in return for help with the chores. She found herself stuck with a young drug dealer who worked out of her house. It took several long months to rid herself of someone she had hoped would be a companion to help her fill the empty space in her life.

Francine, Jackie, and I all reacted differently to our conflicts about space. Francine decided not to share her space until she became less aggravated by others. She hopes someday a toothpaste top left off or a toilet seat left up will no longer send her into an angry fit.

Jackie waited several months before she tried again to fill her empty space. This time she carefully screened candidates for a housemate, interviewing people extensively and checking their references meticulously. She finally settled on a hard-working college student who both did his chores effectively and also provided her with interesting and agreeable companionship.

On my part, I searched for the cause of my dilemma by free-associating: suffocation, smothering, asphyxiation, envelopment, and being overwhelmed. What on earth was all this about? I tried to recall my feelings about sharing space before I had married Leonard, certain that they had been the antithesis of my current feelings. I glided into my marriage visualizing an open and unrestricted picture. I had been living alone and was looking forward to living with someone else. "Space," had I thought of the word then, would have felt expansive, unenclosed, and easy. However, "space" wasn't part of my vocabulary.

Searching my psyche, I reasoned with myself. Why the immense contrast? What had happened? *Loss* was my answer. Equating shared space with the potential for loss, I wandered through my convoluted, involuted thoughts. "You," I said firmly, "keep doors locked so the pain will stay out. If you open them, only destruction can enter." I assured myself I would not take that chance; my wounds had turned into scars that could never be opened again.

Maggie-the-man-hater, still my friend at that point, assured me that I was reacting to my years with Leonard. She said she saw Leonard's life-style as having been excessively demanding of my time and space; she claimed that my feelings were an appropriate, long-delayed reaction. She thought that if Leonard had had his druthers, he would have married a geisha girl or a genie. "All men," she said, "if they told you honestly about their fantasies of what they'd like, would tell you about one or the other or perhaps some disembodied spirit which would meet their every need. Your Leonard was a space-eater."

Maggie was wrong. She had tapped into the fact that space had once been an issue between Leonard and me. In the early years Leonard had been demanding of my time. His concert bookings were global and he wanted me to travel everywhere and be available most of the time. I had jokingly called him the "human vacuum cleaner," which was my way of asking for more room to be on my own. Indirect as I was, Leonard heard me and over the years we managed to work through our problems.

Hearing Maggie describe Leonard as a space-eater made me realize once again the extent of *her* problems. Long ago I had resolved the demands of Leonard's career and knew for certain that he was not causing my present conflict over space. Unshared space was my protection against involvement and the threat of closeness. As long as I concealed myself behind my defensive walls, I would be safe.

Space can be a problem for many people, whether they're widowed or not, but we widows confront specific issues around defining and renegotiating it, especially if we are living in space once shared.

How can we make our homes places in which *we* feel at home—contented, secure, and at peace? Some widows are content to leave things exactly the way they are; others need to make changes. I know a widow who, by moving her furniture around, transformed her bedroom into a comfortable sitting room that she loved to be in. Another widow left her room the way it was but replaced the old bed; seeing it after her husband died made her miserable. A third widow completely redecorated her apartment so that it no longer held painful memories for her.

These were all minor alterations that didn't require major exploration. However, Judy, a patient, had to go through months of therapy before she could change her feelings. Widowed three years, Judy was obsessed with protecting her space. She had put together a life she said she loved, but she was complaining of "void attacks." When I asked her to give me another word for "void," she said "empty" and "unattached."

Judy was frantic about anyone impinging on her space. She had grown up in a family without frames; they had no bounds and knew no limits. No one had any privacy—no locks on the doors, no knocking necessary before entering a room. And no place was sacred—intrusions into bathrooms were a common occurrence. Often Judy's father carried on lengthy conversations from his seat on the toilet while Judy was in her bedroom. She promised herself that her future would include borders and limits.

Soon after becoming an adult, Judy married Tom. He came from a family with similar problems, so together they comfortably defined his and her space, making an unwritten contract that neither would intrude upon the other. It worked.

After Tom's death Judy repressed her panic that her space was at risk. Out of touch with her real feelings, she was rigidly insistent that her lovers not stay the night in her house, even though she was willing to spend the night at theirs. Also, she felt suffocated at home whenever she entertained more than two people at the same time, and inflexibly demanded forty-eight hours' notice for company so she could plan and rehearse their interaction.

I asked Judy what exactly she was afraid might happen if friends impulsively dropped by to see her. She shuddered. "Rude . . . awful . . . I'd be livid! They wouldn't dare."

Judy was right: no one knowing her would have dared move into her space. That was then. Four months later someone who had just met her decided to break through her defenses. Don, a friend of a friend, asked Judy out and later became her lover. Again she tried to distance herself, defining her space and attempting to force him to do the same. He refused to play her game, then terrified her by impulsively showing up at her office to bring her flowers. Reacting like a bear caught in a trap, she assaulted him verbally, screaming and yelling that according to accepted rules offices were off-limits. Don countered that love altered all rules, but Judy didn't agree. She continued to fight, forcing their decision not to see each other anymore. Both sulked for a week; then Judy called him and apologized for her excessive reaction. They reconciled, worked through their differences, and are still sharing what was once only Judy's space.

We're all different, exploring and resolving our space and finding different solutions. I thought all my questions were new, but they weren't. I didn't know that they were questions that I had answered once long ago and now had to reexamine in order to answer them again in my new life.

Intimacy

After space, the next confronting hurdle was figuring out how I felt about intimacy. In August 1986 I attended a conference in Boston where therapists from all over the United States came to discuss experiences with intimacy, a topic increasingly being addressed by our patients.

I reviewed my caseload of patients and found that although not one of them had originally presented the problem, they had all, as they moved forward to deal with conflicted relationships, come face-to-face with their limited capacities for intimate attachments.

The therapists at the conference tried to define the problem and reached the conclusion that "intimacy" was the eighties buzzword for closeness and sex. It provided both therapists and patients with a wastebasket diagnosis into which we could throw a wide range of issues. However, it was clear to me on leaving the conference that "intimacy" was a word to be defined case by case, problem by problem.

I was particularly interested in my widowed patients and paid closer attention to this aspect of their lives. Thirty-six-year-old Deirdre saw herself as feeling free and comfortable with intimacy. She had sex three times a week with three different men. She delighted in their appreciation of her sexuality but experienced no feelings of her own. She was in therapy because her late husband had fought with her through their five years of marriage about her need to lock her emotions away. As we sorted through her life she discovered her fear of emotions was a direct result of her mother's chronic, suffocating demands that they be inseparable—that she and Mama be symbiotically attached permanently.

Louise had been married to Sam, a man who insisted that his possessions not be touched or violated; his chest of drawers, desk, books, closet—all were off-limits to Louise. Although she had been willing to share her possessions with Sam, Louise was unable to enter into an emotional sharing. She couldn't tell him how his behavior had affected her or their life together. However, she could rail at him about his failure to make big money that would have given her the status she desired. Both thought their constant bickering was symptomatic of their closeness, but it wasn't. After Sam died Louise began to explore her problems with intimacy.

Louise and Sam reminded me of my friends Maggie and David, both astoundingly verbal, who heartlessly dissected their feelings. They could extract a feeling from an event, scrutinize it under a microscope, and discuss it endlessly. They had a mesmerizing talent that served them badly, each dissection distancing them further from each other.

Sam and Louise, Maggie and David talked *at* one another, never *to* or *with* one another. Both couples were missing the powerful connection that would have given them the freedom to say exactly what they were feeling. Each avoided anxiety-provoking content by picking on safe topics, communicating in an indirect and destructive fashion. Each had his or her role in the process of drifting apart to their separate and nonintimate places.

Certain people have an innate talent for intimacy, much as others are born talented with a paintbrush or musical instrument. But for most people it's a learned talent, not an entitlement or a birthright. Some, their terror out of control, flee intimacy as if it were the plague. These "distancers," for whom the absence of intimacy means no genuine connection, no profound emotional demand, no need to grow or change with another person, are comfortable with their lifetime guarantee—they will never be asked to share special parts of themselves.

Immediately after Leonard's death I dealt with questions of intimacy professionally, never thinking about it in connection with myself. Now, in a new place, pushed by Norman to push even further, I was reexamining my personal feelings about intimacy. I whispered to myself, "Intimacy, intimacy," as I walked around the city. Had I been good at it? Was it a major part of my relationship with Leonard? We had been comfortably close; he was my most special friend with whom I shared my secrets, my dreams, my fears. We had always found ways to say the things we needed to say without fear of the other's response. Perhaps more leisure time together would have increased our intimacy, but neither of us was good at leisure.

But we had exposed our best and worst selves to each other. We saw each other's nasties and uglies, our neurotic child parts when they surfaced periodically. I recall being in an audience surrounded by fans of Leonard. "He's so cool," they'd say. "How does he do it?" Little could they know what turmoil and sweat had gone into his presentation of a "cool" self. Our connection/intimacy/trust included warts and all. We didn't need to hide.

In *Necessary Losses*, Judith Viorst writes, "To need other people, to help and console you, to share the good times and the bad, to say, 'I understand,' to be on your side—and also to need the reverse, to need to be needed, may lie at the heart of every woman's identity. . . . Identity, for women, has more to do with intimacy than with separateness."

I read that paragraph shortly after Leonard's death, realizing that someday I would reread it. A year later I did, and was staggered by my recognition that a piece of my identity, as a part of a close, loving relationship with a man, was gone.

I wanted that sense of identity back. "But," said the little saboteur resting on my shoulder, "are you willing to pay the price?" Earlier weighty questioning of other subjects now lightened by comparison. My saboteur went at me again. "Are you still capable of real closeness? Are you willing to confide your most private thoughts and listen to someone tell you their most tightly kept secrets?" The vulnerable, fragile part of me, the glue that had attached me to Leonard, had vanished with him.

Again I thought of Sam and Louise. Neither of them had been willing to drop their mask to allow their spouse to see them as they really were. Using techniques learned early in their marriage, they had found different ways to hide their true selves from each other; Louise remained backed against a wall of envy as Sam obsessed about space and limitations. I understood why they had chosen their unique routes of distancing. Despite their pain, hiding felt safer than exposure.

For us widows, intimacy touches that innermost private part of our being. It has many faces and is difficult to confront; therefore it is often denied. Paula, extremely successful as an editor, brilliantly described various ways her colleagues sabotaged their intimate relationships: the games they played; the masks they wore; the major communications breakdowns that resulted. Successful and brilliant as she was, Paula was unable to use her insights on herself. When she told me about her husband, I heard about a marriage in which he and she had made a silent contract to maintain independent lives. They worked around the clock and took separate vacations from each other. As she talked Paula became frantic, exposing a fragile, disassociated woman who described her marriage as "convenient, since I was always able to do my own thing." As for her present life, she was working a sixty-hour week, which she rationalized as her way of keeping in touch with creative people. Actually it was her way of avoiding the threat of intimacy.

Another widow, Nancy, was quick to admit that she had always had problems with intimacy, citing her relationship with her late husband and her children. She had been unable to tolerate confrontations, insisting on an intermediary. She had only been able to deal with her husband and children by using one to talk to the other. Knowing her husband would do her dirty work for her, she told him how and why her children should change certain behaviors. In the same way she used her children: "Tell Daddy I'm unhappy about" this or that.

Nancy had been able to squeeze every drop of intimacy out of these relationships by being interested only in power. Speaking through others gave her a vaunted place in the family structure. At the same time it had cut her off from the intimacy of direct, one-on-one communication.

Now Nancy, widowed four years, was questioning whether power was as important as she had previously thought. She described her new relationship with a man who was demanding that she deal directly with him. He was trying to teach her to express her feelings immediately, instead of either denying or delaying them. She said, "I feel so close to him because he lets me be me . . . it's different but it's great!"

Vickie, a buyer for a department store, said her greatest discovery since the death of her husband was her conflict about intimacy. She had been living with a widower and his two children for nine years. She brought her obsession, jogging, into her relationships to limit intimate contact. The use of an uncontained passionate interest provided a wedge between her and those close to her. She had always been running, literally and symbolically, from the closeness they needed. She realized that she, like them, had been missing a vital piece of the relationship; now she wanted to connect with the widower and his two children in a far more intense way. She was ready to stop running.

Paula wasn't ready to resolve her intimacy conflicts; Nancy and Vickie were. Trying to picture myself in a relationship in which intimacy would be a major part, I wondered where I was going to find my lost talent for it. Would I wear a mask of denial like the workaholic or the runner? Or was I ready for intimacy?

8

Second Chance

Taking Inventory

It's time to take inventory. Wherever you are, whatever you're feeling, you and your situation are different from the way you were during the period immediately following your husband's death. Try to recall the things you did during the day, during the night, your family, your friends, your home, and, most important, your feelings. What was it like to live through each twenty-four hours?

I remember awakening with eyelids as heavy as cement when I forced myself to look at my new and altered reality. A friend said, "I see feeble old women in the street and all I can picture is my miserable life staying the way it is now until I end up where they are." I knew exactly how she felt.

My forever had stretched ahead of me, lonely, empty, an endless road to nowhere. Life was frozen and would stay the way it was. Not having taken inventory I couldn't see the profound effect the turning points had made on both my way of living and on my growth. Changes create new changes, which made it imperative for me to take a harsh, direct look at different pieces of my life, some of which were working, some of which weren't.

For me, the area that needed the harshest exploration was friends. They required and deserved profound consideration. Some "friends" were no longer an issue. The music world, never too proficient at dealing with relatives of its stars, severed most of its ties with me. Yo-Yo Ma and Leonard's manager were comforting exceptions, but other colleagues and friends dropped from sight as immediately as if we had suddenly begun inhabiting different planets.

This experience was shared by my friend Paula, who had been married to a respected television producer. After he died, she was devastated when his colleagues, whom she had thought of as friends, didn't write or call. Mary, another friend, brooded for over a year after her husband died because his closest partner in his law firm didn't get in touch with her.

Paula, Mary, and I suffered much more than the loss of a so-called friend. We also lost our connections to our husband's professions, so much a part of them and a remaining tie for us. These friends disappeared, taking with them a world we had treasured.

The loss of friends continued to gnaw away at me much of the time. Why were so many intense friendships gone from my life? Reviewing my losses I tried to find the reasons but couldn't explain away my pain caused by the absence of those friends.

My feelings of betrayal felt as sharp as they had felt in the beginning when, immediately after Leonard's death, some friends disconnected and withdrew from my life. I hated my hurt and hated not being able to forget my vanished friends.

I checked with other widows to find out if they, like me, still felt so raw about their lost connections. Vera's closest friends had become totally inaccessible to her because, they said, she didn't fit into their world of couples. Vera became teary as she talked about her absent friends—she wasn't ready to let them go either.

Betsy had a different view. She said she couldn't care less. *All* her friends from the past except one had deserted her, but she claimed it was their loss, not hers.

I hoped eventually I would feel like Betsy, but for now I had to stop thinking about my losses and begin to think about the destructive remainders: friends who had stayed but who needed to be reassessed in my new existence.

I began with my decaying relationship with Maggie, still a major force in my life to whom I had clung despite my increasing strength and awareness of her negative influence. "Primitive, early infantile impairment" was the way a colleague put it when she found herself trapped in a decomposing friendship of long standing. Wondering about my relationship with Maggie, I asked this colleague, "Your impairment or hers?" "Both," she said, "but I should be ready to come in out of the rain."

Why couldn't she? Why couldn't I? Why were we stuck with our baby stuff when clearly it was time to grow up?

Maggie, always heading straight for the negative, first to undermine change and growth, eternally denying kindness or goodness by overanalyzing every transaction, was still my friend. I had watched her swallow up David, destroy a business partner, and undermine colleagues without realizing she was doing the same to me. I had assumed that the uniqueness of our relationship would have brought out the best in her and felt protected as I witnessed her poison taking effect on everyone else. She watched as I became stronger and at every better turn she devalued my good feelings. "You're less anxious than you were . . . is it because you've given up hope?" "Don't tell me you had a good time at the party—you were either drunk or desperate." Pretending to be supportive, she went on carping. But at last I began really hearing her, and understood that destruction was the name of her game.

Robin, a patient, was also holding on to an old friendship that was reinforcing her negative feelings. Her childhood friend Barbara reported daily on their mutual acquaintances' comments about her appearance. "Ann thinks you're too thin for a woman your age," she related, hitting Robin twice in one sentence. "You'll need a new image," Barbara quoted another acquaintance, "but be sure not to drift too far from your square, preppy look . . . you'll be unrecognizable . . ." Smash, bang—a blow to the ego that reinforced all of Robin's frailty.

It was easy for me to see that Robin was at risk, but much harder to admit that I too was stuck in a harmful friendship.

Maggie's wasn't the only disabling voice; others were reluctant to support my emerging spirit. "Travel alone? Are you crazy?" "Oh, you moved . . . so soon! What about your friends? And what if you have a change of heart after spending all that money?" "Learn to ski? At your age? Why, you'll maim yourself for life!"

Weakening, thwarting, impoverishing expressions surround us all. Cliff's daughter humiliated him for his courageous attempt at cooking. Vera's sister repeatedly belittled her excitement about returning to school: "You a student?

Ha! You barely made it through high school." Francine, Betsy's longtime friend, interpreted her work on behalf of widows as "wasted time." Maggie, going straight for my jugular, told me that Leonard's death had negatively affected my professional judgments. But when I asked her in what way, she was unable to give me an example and lamely said, "Well, you're so busy changing, something has to go wrong professionally."

Maggie was the thing that had gone wrong, and so she had to go. During one of our intense conversations I finally told her we needed to take a break from each other. Unlike Vera's and Cliff's, my debilitating figure wasn't a relative, so getting her out of my life required minor surgery rather than an amputation.

Maggie agreed to the break, but not without sending me off with a sizable list of my inadequacies with which I was now to face life.

Taking inventory guarantees a healthy, constructive support system. By sharpening our perceptions, it allows us to differentiate instantaneously between people who will sustain our growth and people who will stunt or destroy it. We all know people who collect trigger sentences to whip out and create instant panic when we're under pressure. The Maggies of the world are weak-spot collectors, intuitively opening sores that haven't healed. A Maggie innocently says, "Do you ever worry about getting sick in the middle of the night when you're all alone?" And of course a Maggie chooses the precise moment when you're worrying about it to ask the question. Maggies are always at the front line of negative voices, just waiting to talk about anxiety-provoking subjects.

By reinforcing my fears, Maggie validated her role as the

acting, strong, all-knowing parent. As long as she maintained her status, Maggie blocked out her own fears, her own unresolved issues—and most of all, her own life, which was tumbling down around her.

Taking our inventory periodically is a necessity in moving forward; it guarantees us a healthy, constructive support system to encourage growth into the next period of our lives. Take a second look at the people on whom you rely for corroboration and reinforcement. Examine their capacities for joy, fun, and excitement—they affect you. Are they responsive to your positive attitudes and reactions, or do they respond only when you weep and brood about your hopelessness and fears? How often do they say, "Yes, but . . ." or "If only you'd . . ." or "You shouldn't . . ." Some friends love you stuck where you are and as you are, and may let you know by actually saying so or by nonverbal communication (shoulders hunched, eyebrow raised, body turned away), telling you they're available only when you're down. They may not know they're doing it, so it's useful to negotiate with them by saying how you're experiencing their behavior. Many can and will change. More can't and don't want to. You'll recognize who your healthy-making friends are, and you'll keep them. The rest, the Maggies, have to go—it's time to sort out and clean up.

Sorting Out
and Cleaning Up

Using a scale of 1 to 10, rate your troubling relationship in the second column and add up the total. Insert the name of your "Maggie" in the questions.

1. Do you feel uncomfortable more often than less often with _____ ? _____

2. Are you usually concerned with your physical appearance when preparing to be with _____ ? _____

3. Do you find yourself hearing an old and inappropriate tape when you're with _____ ? _____

4. Do you feel less competent after you've spent an evening with _____ ? _____

5. Can you visualize your life without _____ ? _____

6. Are you afraid to reevaluate the status of your relationship with _____ ? _____

7. Picture the two of you ten years from now. Is it possible for you to see that life is better for you than it is for _____ ? _____

TOTAL _____

If your total is above 35, it's time to renegotiate your friendship. If it's 50 or over, it's time to get tough and clean up by terminating the relationship.

The Importance of Hugging

Euphoric about my intention to rid my life of destructive "Maggies," I shared my decision with the group. Although everyone thought it a constructive step, some were afraid to let go of *any* friends, since they had so few. Then Norman announced that he was decreasing his social life, saying he'd had enough dating to last him the rest of his life. He too was going to be more selective and planned to concentrate on his work and socialize with just a couple of friends. He talked about his decision in a disconnected voice that lacked its usual vibrant, haughty sound. Seeming defeated and sad, he reminded me of a child who discovers that there is no Santa and is wondering if there still is an Easter Bunny.

It made me anxious to listen to him sounding totally unlike the Norman I knew so well. The group wanted to explore the reasons for his change but we were distracted by Norman's denial that anything was different. Cliff finally was able to shed some light on events in Norman's life, since the two of them kept each other up to date on their social programs. For several months Norman had been seeing a widow with whom he was impressed and delighted. She felt the same way about him but had let him know from the very beginning that sexual contact with anyone was out of the question. Norman had accepted this arrangement by assuming that it would quickly change, confident that he would be the exception that broke this widow's rule. When things didn't go as he had expected, he issued an ultimatum: "You have a month to get your act together—then I split, run, am gone." The month passed, as did another two months, with no change. Norman became despondent.

Clare, the widow in question, had been alone a year before meeting Norman. Her husband, Eric, had died during a minor surgical procedure as a result of an allergic reaction to the anesthesia. Still in enormous pain over his death, Clare had forced herself to go to a party at which she met Norman.

Clare wasn't ready to be at a party—and she was far less ready for Norman—yet she was in a place where she could acknowledge the past pleasure she'd gotten from men. Norman, despite his brash, frontal approach, was appealing, charming, and bright. She had agreed to see him on the condition there would be no conflict about sex. She was eons away from being ready even to think about being ready.

As Cliff explained Norman's situation, I could sense the group's collective wariness. Nonfeeling Norman, love-'em-and-leave-'em, bon vivant Norman, Ph.D. of the bedroom, was actually showing us a different side of himself, and by doing so was leading us once more to a need for another reevaluation of ourselves. If he was showing soft spots that would help him reconnect out there in the world of singles, maybe we had them too, and could also reconnect.

I began thinking about the previous Sunday night, when I had a blind date with a widower arranged by a mutual friend. Both of us confessed that we were initially appalled by the terminology "blind date"/"widow"/"widower," but the words quickly receded into oblivion as we settled down to getting acquainted. Our common loss seemed to make us more sensitive and in tune with each other, and we spent a delightful evening talking primarily about our past lives.

The evening had ended after Warren the Widower (as I christened him) asked for and received a hug. I was astonished by his request, having heard repeatedly that the major difference between men and women following the death of a spouse was their preference for physical contact. Men were purportedly interested in sex whereas women wanted only to be held and caressed. Here was Warren, a man who needed and wanted exactly what I needed and wanted.

We talked about hugging and decided it was the warmest, softest, most nurturing activity. We agreed that it made us feel safe and protected. After Warren left I reviewed my associations with hugs and decided that the best medicine on earth is a good hug. It reminded me of a time without pain or fear, a place where there was no anxiety. In the group, I was compelled to ask Norman his views on hugging, suspecting he would hate the question. He called me a "plate of mush" and demanded to know why I was asking. Telling of my experience, I suggested that his Clare might respond in the same way.

The "hug" question opened up a discussion that created one of our best group meetings. Vera talked about her experience with a cold, uncaring man with whom she had been briefly involved. He was of the "no touch" school, interested only in the sexual act. In ending the relationship Vera had told him, "I'm interested in making love, not making sex!" Puzzled, he told her she was never going to find whatever it was she was talking about. Everyone laughed except Cliff, who commented soberly that he was now ready for a serious relationship but the women he was meeting were of the free-spirit variety, much as he had been up until now.

Norman, at first astonished, now seemed more ill at ease. Pressing Cliff, he asked him to elaborate on the exact requirements he now had. Cliff said he wanted closeness, not performance, and added, "A hug from someone I'm really close to makes me feel as if I could lift the world with one hand."

The women in the group looked at one another expecting to find dissension and confrontation, but we were all nodding in agreement. The only one out of sync was Norman, who had been forced by Clare to question his sex appeal and his previously irresistible charm.

Sybil asked Norman if he thought Clare might be worth waiting for. Perhaps as she got to know him better, she would be less frightened and more open to a broader relationship.

Norman said he didn't want to waste his life *waiting*, and besides . . .

He seemed unwilling to continue but Cliff pushed him on and discovered Norman's reluctance to become further involved with Clare's "neurosis." Norman said, "I had one neurotic woman to deal with for years and that's enough."

"Neurotic like what?" we demanded. "Like what?"

Norman glanced down at his watch, annoyed to find we had loads of time left. He then talked about Clare's difficulty in letting go of her late husband—her struggle to remove his remaining clothing from the closet and her preoccupation with unfinished business at the hospital where he had died.

Individually and loudly we pointed out to Norman that he was calling Clare neurotic for feelings and behavior all of us had experienced. Curious, Betsy wanted to know the connection between Clare's burgeoning neurosis and our discussion about hugging.

Furious, Norman accused us of nit-picking and trying to embarrass him. He announced that the group had become preachy, boring, and essentially nonsupportive. He was, he said, thinking about quitting the group. We knew we had him: Norman barked loudest when he was most troubled. We pressed on, leading and supporting Norman to a place where he could talk about hugs and hugging. We discovered that as a child he had never been picked up and hugged by either of his parents. They were smart, highly educated, cold people who followed the dictum of their times: "Don't touch children, it's unhealthy." And so Norman had grown up without hugs.

I had a sudden revelation about why Norman and I had spent so much time fighting each other. Unconsciously we had recognized similar traits. Having been brought up the same way as Norman, I had only as an adult learned to hug and flourish in a world of warmth that hugs provide. Obviously he and I had a lot in common, but I was way ahead of him. Walking on eggshells, I suggested to the group that we teach Norman how to hug.

"Dumb idea," he grumbled, but the group pretended not to hear him. His body language implored, "Teach me, teach me."

We role-played, taking turns being different people of different ages, until it was Norman's turn—first to be hugged, then to hug. We asked him what age he wanted to pretend to be, and he answered, "Four." So we hugged our needy four-year-old. He delighted in each and every contact, giggling self-consciously at first, but finally relaxing into the moment. Then it was time for him to choose someone he wanted to hug. The group waited silently as he made his way around the table. We were all surprised when he stopped in front of Betsy, who hadn't been hugged in years. When he gave her a huge, delicious bear hug, I knew he was ready to return to Clare—to give and receive many more comforting hugs. Perhaps their relationship had a future; perhaps it did not. Whatever the outcome, the group, as always, had made at least one of its members think differently from the way he or she ever had before.

I smiled to myself, thinking about the group. We had come so far in such a short time, dropping many defenses and letting one another into our most carefully guarded places. I realized my fellow group members knew me better than did most of my friends. I was unable to picture one person now in my life, sitting for an hour and a half as the group had, talking about hugging. Or was I? My Saturday night blind date, "Warren the Widower," just might have loved it.

Protect and Defend

My circle of widows was now sizable. Widows know widows and are sociable with one another. My network had expanded and adapted to new recruits, broadening my social life and adding to my experiences.

Tina called to tell me she was moving to California to live with a man she had met on a trip. She went on at length about her friends' negative reactions to her decision—"He's too old," or "He's a bit creepy," and "It'll be a major mistake." She thought he was wonderful and wanted me to meet him and give her my opinion.

She asked about my work and social life. I told her nothing was new; that life was peaceful and unexciting. Symbolically we took each other's temperature from time to time to determine mental health and the state of our mourning. We discovered we had each moved into a vital new life, instead of existing in limbo. We had both been widowed about two years, moving through the blackest, deepest pain into our new reality. No one had prepared us for our transition; we had limped, stumbled, and dragged our broken spirits through one day at a time. Like a brand-new pair of shoes that pinch until the leather softens and becomes comfortable, our *new* lives had simply become our *lives*. Everything was in place; my home, my friends, my sense of self were altered but comfortable. I thought about Leonard frequently, but now I thought about him within my new framework; *my* life, not *our* life.

My friend Tina and I were like war buddies, having shared our most desperate moments. She sounded certain that life in California would be right for her. How could she contemplate an additional transition after the trauma of widowhood and all the adjustments she had been forced to make? Why didn't she sound the slightest bit frightened or insecure? "I'm not," she insisted when I asked her. "I'm no longer scared of anything."

I told her I was equally sanguine and fearless. But she didn't answer, which made me wonder if she knew something I didn't. I felt fearless, yet knew myself well enough to know I had put together one of the great defense systems of all times, a defense system so powerful that it could cut me off from knowing for sure whether I was afraid or not. I had thought I was stronger, with fewer defenses, that generally I was in touch with my fears and anxieties. But I was wrong.

I called several widows, ostensibly to check on their reactions to Tina's adaptive capacities. What I desperately wanted was some feedback about *my* lack of adaptability.

I had told Tina several untruths. When I described my social life as unexciting I had neatly bypassed Warren, who, since our first night's hug, had been in my life and in my hair. And in my bed. In truth I found I wasn't afraid of anything—as long as I maintained total control of the anything. Tina's move fazed me only on a subconscious level; consciously I couldn't relate to it. It was so foreign that to me it was a nonevent.

This was more than I could say of Warren. He was someone who threatened everything I cherished. He demanded time, care, space (without knowing what it was called), interaction, and, above all, a receptacle of his kindness and generosity. Despite the recent death of his wife, to whom he had been devoted for forty years, he seemed psychologically intact. Her loss was causing him intense pain, something I could totally identify with. But he appeared far less injured and fragile than I had been at the same period after Leonard's death. I was convinced that his wife's death had not yet fully hit him and that his reaction was still to come.

I discussed our different reactions with friends and colleagues, who assured me that I was wrong to expect men to react the same way that women did to their spouse's death. A few of my colleagues backed up their theory that men comfortably and quickly establish new relationships, feeling no guilt toward their spouses, by citing a Glick, Parks, and Weiss study of 1975. Glick *et al.* agreed that women needed to work through their feelings of being disloyal before they could reconnect. As Betsy said again and again, "Women mourn, men replace."

A colleague told me about her widowed patient Marion, who emotionally supported her best friend's husband through his wife's terminal illness. Marion, a widow of four years, went daily to the hospital to sit and wait with Mike. She brought food and ran errands; mostly she offered him understanding and shared feelings. After her friend's funeral, Mike and Marion phoned each other often, checking on how each was doing. Mike confessed he couldn't have gotten through his wife's death without her aid. After a year, he suggested they share a house together. Marion said she preferred marriage to just living together, and so they were wed.

My reaction to the Mike-Marion relationship was nearly as negative as my reaction to Warren's intensity. I interpreted their marriage as a convenient arrangement and, sounding like my women's lib friends, I blustered about men's dependency—women were far better able to take care of themselves than men, who were incapable of running a house, taking charge of social transactions, or dealing with their children. The speed with which men like Mike remarried was proof that there had been a major mix-up in the old saw that said women were the weaker sex.

Increasingly I heard stories that reinforced my views. A

friend called to report that her doctor, a widower of four months, had told her he felt ready to meet a woman; she hoped I was ready to meet a man. Three weeks later she called back to say forget it—her doctor had already met someone else. Both friends and colleagues knew examples of men's speedy recovery from their loss. Frank, after a good marriage of twenty-eight years, met a woman on the commuter train two months after his wife's death. They became sexually involved almost immediately and moved in together after six weeks. Again I characterized his impetuous behavior as proof of a man's need to have someone fetch his dry cleaning and be sure there was food in the fridge. And again I retreated further behind my barrier of superiority and certainty of my independence.

As a result of their desperation, Mike, Tina, Marion, and Frank were choosing to live with someone, anyone, rather than live alone. Warren pleasantly but firmly disagreed. He interpreted their decisions to live together as a healthy need to be part of another person's life. He was unimpressed with the priority I placed on independence and my determination to prove I could live alone. "Why would you *want* to?" he asked.

I told him about my uphill fight after Leonard died, how I had felt like a cripple learning to walk again as I tried putting together a life of my own. Now I was a puzzle finally feeling whole and connected after fitting back together the pieces that had been me. This newly defined me told Warren all about my identity and about my need for space. Acting as if he had never heard the term before, he asked me for an explanation of "space."

I couldn't tell him that he threatened to take away a place that, because I had set new rules, now felt safe and comfortable. Instead I suggested that he demanded too much time that interfered with my growth and development. The new, free me, I explained, was planning to take courses in computers and astrology as part of an expanding widow's life. He responded by suggesting he move into my apartment, saying we could grow and develop together.

After a five-minute screaming fit, I told him we were incompatible and that he should leave. He did—but returned an hour later. He found me subdued but still at odds with what I considered his intrusive behavior. Slowly and carefully we reconciled our different attitudes toward the relationship to the point where we could continue to see each other. However, I remained alert and on guard, recalling Betsy's collection of endless statistics. Warren was a threat to my self-assurance. Statistical fact: widowers remarry. The U.S. Census Bureau figures show, in the fifty-five to sixty-four age range, eighty percent of men are married, compared to seventy percent of women. As the age range increases, the numbers radically change. In the sixty-five to seventy-four age bracket, eighty-one percent of the men are married, but only fifty percent of the women. Betsy may have had the numbers right but she didn't know the pain behind the numbers. A divorced patient of mine married a widower who would not permit her to move any of the furniture in the house he had shared with his first wife. My patient lived in a mausoleum of old photographs and memorabilia of another wife and another's life. His late wife had spent her last months in a wheelchair, and the widower would not allow his new wife to remove the tracks still showing on the floor. It was a hopeless situation and two years later their marriage ended.

I told Warren about this disastrous marriage and cited more evidence of the calamity of precipitous remarrying. I was astonished to realize that, negative as I was about the

subject, *I* was the one bringing it up. Why was it so important to me? I sensed major danger to my new solitary life.
Death had struck, leaving in its wake a battle for survival
that I had only recently won. I was a victorious woman who
now could do things I'd never contemplated before. Like so
many widows I knew, I had unwillingly become stronger as
a result of loss. Warren wouldn't, perhaps couldn't, understand this. I decided to continue down the road with my
mouth shut, hardly noticing that my commitment to aloneness had already begun to erode.

Taking Risks

I was articulate about my need for independence but mute
about my fears. This stance protected me from addressing
my most vulnerable healing but not yet healed injuries. I
talked freely about my newly discovered strengths but
never about my weaknesses. Like most widows I knew, I
wanted a man in my life, but on a limited basis. I talked
about "wanting a man just to have dinner with—a key person to offset the stifling totality of a female world." Betty, a
patient, spoke longingly of "a man who will take my arm
crossing the street." Rita missed seeing "pipes and tobacco
around the house." All three of us liked men but . . . Never
again would we go through so wrenching a loss. In time,
after Leonard's death, I had managed to survive the loss of
my most intimate conspirator, my caretaker and protector,
my best friend and lover, all at one time. I had also lost a
life-style, periodically difficult but one that was mostly glam-
orous and exciting. Internally and externally everything had
changed and become different. I was more independent,

more sociable, more tolerant, and more integrated. My home, my friends, and my world had radically changed. Little by little I had climbed out of a pit into my new life. Nothing would threaten me or that new life ever again.

Tina and Claudia, both willing to commit themselves to new and permanent relationships, appeared to be at risk. Tina, having lost her husband only three years earlier, had begun a new life in which she was now settled. Once again she was starting over, moving west to a new life, prepared to begin again.

Claudia, my young widowed friend with her two teenage daughters and her new lover, would have to negotiate a new way not only with her daughters but also with her new love's only child, an overpossessive daughter.

However, I found myself far more comfortable hearing from widows like Betty, who refused to move into new, committed relationships. Betty was straightforward with her adamant declaration, "Never again will I find myself having to take care of a sick man . . . I've paid my dues . . . once is enough. I gave up my life for Tom, living in death's shadow for nine months, and it won't happen again, ever."

I was reminded of my doll Ruthie. When I was eight she tumbled from our fifth-floor window and broke into small pieces. My mother took her to the doll hospital to be glued back together again. The doll doctor told my mother to caution me to be extra careful in the future. "Next time," he warned, "I won't be able to fix her, the pieces will be too tiny. It will be impossible to fit them together again." I, like Ruthie, could become unfixable if broken twice.

I knew many widows with similar concerns who were involved in safe, time-limited relationships. They carefully chose men whom they were certain wouldn't make serious demands. Rita had been involved briefly with two married men to whom she freely devoted herself, confident in the knowledge that they belonged to other women. Frances chose a man with an excessively dependent mother whose forceful requirements precluded any permanent relationship.

Other widows resolved their fear of loss by choosing men they knew were inappropriate, men who could never fit into their lives. A blatant example was Della, who spent the first two years after she was widowed with men so dependent on her that she knew she would be the one to leave. Hanging on her financially, emotionally, and psychologically, each man made her feel secure and safe in the knowledge that her one loss, the loss of her husband, would be her only loss.

Women sometimes become professional widows—Mrs. So-and-So, wife of the talented and famous Somebody who died eons ago. She is still the wife of, defined by him—his talent, his position, his status, much the same way she had been defined when he was alive. My patient Joanna, when offered the love and companionship of a lawyer whom she adored, asked, "How can I give up the prestige and power paid to the wife of a famous man to be the wife of a nobody?" First she had to learn the difference between her living man and her living legend. But even then she chose the leftover life of fame rather than a new life with an unexalted man.

The widow of a famous musician devoted her life to enshrining her late husband by attending all the musical events where he was honored. She made speeches, had statues commissioned, and arranged for testimonials. Memorials were repeatedly dedicated to her icon husband; she became a traveling monument.

Were these widows scared of more loss? Or were they

making their decisions fearlessly and wisely? Was I like them? Did I feel safer as Widow Famous than as a woman attached to a living, loving, noncelebrity?

I had assumed that my work to overcome my fears was over, never realizing that it was an ongoing struggle. Now I found new fears. My first reaction was to deny them; my second was to run away. I was bombarded daily by Warren, who insisted on introducing me to his family and friends. We spent long hours on the telephone sharing our separate activities and planning our time together. I felt split in two—one part of me loved it, the other phoned friends to complain that Warren was too intrusive, too pushy, too clingy, and too controlling. In addition, he was being "too nice"! He seemed content to deal with the two parts of me, which came and went as the months passed by. Then a friend suggested I meet her recently widowed cousin. It was the farthest thing from my mind but the occasion opened up topics of discussion between the two parts of me. Was I supposed to go out only with Warren? Was I "allowed" to see other men? Did I want to? If not, what exactly did it mean? Was our relationship a permanent one?

I panicked and called Warren. I said we needed to talk. When we met, I told him he should be seeing other women besides me. I artfully pointed out his recent widowerhood, suggesting that he was still far too vulnerable to be involved in a single relationship; to heal he needed many women in his life. When he disagreed, I urged him to listen to his senior partner in mourning—Xenia knew better. We both needed variety and noncommitment.

It was an issue on which we could not agree. I stuck to my proposal that both of us see other people, which for me remained only a proposal. The inequity between a man's and a woman's opportunities for a social life was played out while I waited. Warren, because of my insistence, asked his friends to introduce him to other women. In less than a week he had a date with Marissa.

The night Warren went out with Marissa, his first date since meeting me, I kept my mushrooming anxiety to myself. One by one, my theories, my excuses, and my fears were replaced by my concern that I had probably destroyed a special, irreplaceable relationship. Forcing Warren into a date he had no interest in, I was at risk—we were at risk. Suddenly I was aware of how much I didn't want him to meet someone else with whom he might have an important relationship.

"Damn it," I heard myself say, "how could you be so careless!" Careless was the word, and insensitive, and stupid! I had set myself up to lose rather than work through my conflicts about us. I tried to mobilize the lessons of my anti-men friends as well as those of women who had resolved their conflicts by deciding to stay alone. But nothing materialized except a replay in my head of the wonderful, nurturing times I'd been having over the past months. "Idiot," I berated myself further, "you allowed your fears to take over; you let go."

By midnight I was frantic. I called Warren's house and found him home, safe, and very angry with me. He had wasted an evening with a beautiful, divorced young woman who bored him to distraction with tales of her analyst, her accountant, her lawyer, and her stingy ex-husband. I wanted to hear it all, especially the parts about her youth and beauty. By the time his anger had abated, we were even closer than before my neurotic self had won over my healthy self. It would never happen again in that particular form.

New into Newer

My saboteur had done its best to demolish our relationship, but luck and Marissa had me triumph in the end. Warren and I were back together and I now stopped pontificating. We were happy as a couple as we continued to preserve our past contacts—a past consisting of our long married lives and our more recent pasts following our losses.

As we attempted to combine our lives, we began to trip over obstacles. First came the children. Clearly more than a passing date, each of us was introduced to the other's family as "a friend." They were adults with families of their own. I watched Leonard's daughter, then Warren's three children, all confronting a new presence in their lives. It was instant panic as they pictured someone else, a stranger, in their deceased parent's role. Too soon . . . oh, my God . . . what if . . . ? What could it mean . . . ? These were the non-verbal communications included in all transactions—eyes wide, heads bent, voices questioning. Was their parent more interested in someone new than in the grandchildren or, worse, in themselves?

My patient Ann shed some light on their dilemma. She had married a widower with two adult children soon after his wife's death. He had convinced Ann that together they could handle anything. On her wedding day she found herself the object of her new stepchildren's acting-out fury at their father's hasty remarriage. He was too important to them to risk outright confrontation; he might abandon them, as their mother had by dying. So they turned their rage on their stepmother. They criticized everything she did—her taste in clothes, the way she furnished the house, how she spent money, the fact that she was a career woman. Seeking support from her husband, Ann soon found that he was more interested in his children's reactions than in hers. All of his pleasant forecasts about his children adjusting to his marriage turned out to be false. However, Ann did not wait long before she issued an ultimatum: "Either this stops or I go." Their real marriage began with that ultimatum.

Ann, like all new people entering old established systems, had to learn that children threatened by change will react. Generally children who have lost a parent have gained a strong role in the remaining parent's life, which they are reluctant to abdicate.

Leonard's daughter strove to be loving and considerate, both wanting me to have a man in my life and profoundly not wanting any intrusion on Leonard's memory. She was also protective of our valuable relationship, which had flourished when I was left on my own.

Warren's children, adoring their father, were concerned at the speed with which he was now presenting a new lady. Briefly they had become his singular interest: Daddy was available as a full-time caretaker, baby-sitter, and pal. Suddenly he was far less available.

Warren and I talked about our children's reactions, admitting our mutual impatience with having to handle them. Following so much heaviness and despair, it seemed like an unnecessary new burden. My childish fantasy was that everyone from our separate worlds would immediately and joyously embrace an addition. But my experience as an adult was that people more often than not react strangely when you least expect them to. My group proved to be no exception.

I talked about Warren, hoping for an enthusiastic and supportive response. I was shattered as one by one they pulled away. Cliff changed the subject, wanting to report on his daughter's latest rebellious behavior; overlooking Warren's importance to me, Norman suggested I was now ready to broaden my dating life. Betsy didn't respond at all; Vera said people Warren's and my ages shouldn't take on serious entanglements because our chances of a second loss were very high. Again I tried to provoke a positive discussion but came up with more indifference. Why had things changed so drastically? I asked Sybil what was causing the bizarre reaction. "Maybe," she answered slowly, "it's because you were the one who didn't want what we wanted, and you ended up with it."

I wondered if she was right. Is it really about envy? And how was the group's reaction related to other negative reactions going on all around us? Warren's late wife had many close friends who were shocked and angry at my appearance so soon after she died; they needed more time to mourn. But, like my patient's stepchildren, they couldn't show their anger appropriately. They couldn't get angry at Warren, who they thought was moving too quickly. Instead they took it out on me, subtly letting me know I didn't belong in their cozy little world. On the other hand, their husbands were warm and generous to us, wishing us well and welcoming me. Unfortunately their behavior fueled their wives' concern that their husbands, faced with a similar loss, might behave exactly as Warren had.

Everyone seemed to be protecting his or her turf. Even my precious Persian Himalayan, Owl, reacted immediately and negatively. The first time Warren stayed overnight, Owl left messy messages, one in the hall and another on, of all places, Warren's pillow. Distraught, I called the vet to find out why Owl, who had never failed to use her litter box, was now dropping on the rug and a pillow. Concerned, the vet asked if Owl's diet had been changed . . . or if her litter box had been moved. "No, no, no," I answered, intensely worried now that Owl might be seriously ill. Then he asked,

"Mrs. Rose, if I recall correctly, you are a widow?" "Yes," I said, not knowing what was coming. "Have you by any chance, Mrs. Rose, changed anything in your, uh, living arrangements?" When I told him Warren had spent the night, he said in a serious voice that cats, like people, protect their world any way they can against intruders. Owl and I had lived totally alone since her arrival at my home and she clearly took a dim view of any change.

Owl's reaction was symbolic of a universal response to change. "Every action has a reaction," every relationship is part of a system that will change as the relationship changes. Leonard and I had a world that drastically altered after Leonard died. I had to start again. Now my new world would change as it dealt with Warren and me. Once again I was in a major transition in which the pieces of my life either fit or didn't fit together.

My widowed friends had warned me. Tina, having decided to remarry, was faced with her solid network of widows, assembled over a lengthy period of time. Her decision to marry left them feeling neglected and angry. She was a turncoat, they implied. "You were one of us and now you're going to the other side." Tina needed and valued their friendship and had to negotiate a new and different connection with those friends who could handle her decision to marry.

Like Tina, I was concerned that my new friends not feel that they were only transitional—friends until the real thing came along. I too wanted them to stay a part of my life. Some did, some didn't. Their decisions appeared to be based more on what was happening in their lives than on what was happening in mine.

Sally, after seven years of being a widow, decided to become part of a couple and found her friends ill at ease with her new mate. Girl talk, anti-man talk, and widow comradery went out the window. Thinking her new mate was the problem, she set up a time to see her friends alone, assuming it would be the way it had always been. She was astonished to find that she and her friends had little to share. How could it happen so fast? Once more she experienced the loss of friends she had felt close to.

Actions cause reactions and changes are actions. Like Sally I had difficulty, but I was finally coming to terms with the reality that friends, except for the remarkable few, are not for all seasons. They are for a particular, limited time or duration. Few will move from one framework into a new one.

As my anxiety dissipated, I found myself filled with new and bubbling energy. Chores that had previously been too difficult to undertake I now tackled easily. My work hours intensified despite my playing much of the night. Energy stimulated activity; activity produced more energy. I felt free and less concerned with people's responses to my new changing life. However, there was one person's reactions that I still needed.

Asking Permission

MY LETTER

Dear Leonard,

It's been ages since I've needed to have a dialogue with you, but certain events have pushed me into writing this letter.

You used to call me a scrapper and a fighter who could come back from every defeat. You were right. I feel as if the road I've been traveling since your death has reached an important intersection. I see roads ahead which turn right or left, all of which seem to offer more growth in my healthy, restructured life. I no longer spend time aching for my old self and the life that went with it. Instead, each new road offers a regeneration filled with infinite possibilities.

I am having trouble saying what I need to say, so let me be direct. Warren wants to marry me, scaring me out of my sensible wits. I don't want to say no but I'm terrified to say yes. As you know, before I met Warren and for months after, I swore that I would never remarry. I wanted men, sure, as friends, dinner companions, maybe even as lovers, but I defined marriage as me being married to *you!* Others might remarry, but never, ever me.

Now, as I attempt to picture me married again, I can see a dim outline that's filled with unanswered questions. Remarriage would mean both starting a new life with someone and also taking on his prior life. Between Warren and me we have so much past baggage I can't imagine how it would all fit. His home, my home; his friends, my friends; his furniture, my furniture; his career, my career; and his children, my children, and our various emotional commitments. We've already experienced an uncomfortable preview from our separate world's reactions to each other's existence. No doubt if we married the reactions would escalate and intensify.

But that's not my major concern. I panic whenever I think of letting go of you in a way that will force me to connect *totally* with someone else. I didn't have to face my panic as long as I lived my life separate from Warren's. I wasn't committed to him or to the relationship in a way that marriage would demand. But Warren has little use for my chatter about living peacefully together without being married; my free-spirited yammering about modern couples who live successfully together without a marriage license leaves him cold. He is articulate and clear about wanting a relationship in which two people care enough about each other to marry. He constantly uses the word "commitment," a word that I never had trouble accepting before Warren, but a word that now sends shivers through my body every time I hear it.

Fearless Warren. He knows what he wants and denies the possibility of risk. I adore everything I know about him but focus primarily on what I don't know. I imagine potential dangers lurking beneath our happiness. Why am I afraid I might be making a mistake? Why am I scaring myself with fears of failure? Why is my greatest fear a repetition of loss, which I doubt I could survive? I tell myself I'm being ridiculous because married or unmarried, the loss of Warren would be a second death of a profoundly loved mate. I tell this to myself, but I guess I'm not listening.

Writing to you helps clarify my muddled feelings. There is something else rattling around amongst my emotions. Childish? Overdependent? I confess to both, acknowledging that I am looking for your permission to close the door on a particular part of our marriage. I need to let go of the we/us part that would be required to make another relationship work. The

rest of you is and always will be a treasured part of
me that goes everywhere I go. Warren and I talk a lot
about you and about his late wife. It's safe and comfortable to bring both of you into our lives; it's fun
sharing our stories about the long journey to our
present existence. For months I wondered how some
of my widowed friends were able to combine their
past and present lives—living with a new relationship as they mourned the loss of an old one. Now I
see that our past lives shape our present lives, helping us move on. Sometimes they have nothing in
common, but other times we hear one say, "You remind me of my husband or wife—you sound exactly
the same." It all fits together—we are the present and
the past.

We are happy. There's laughter, playing, and the
comfortable security that comes from knowing we
each have an important someone rooting for us.
There's a sharing of secrets, concerns, fears, and anxieties, and a resolution of previously unsolvable problems. Released from the crushing grip that depression
had on me, my energy level has never been higher.
There are so many roads. Tell me, do I go by myself or
do I go with Warren?

I revel in my new awareness. You left me with
infinite strengths. You pushed, encouraged, and saw
to it that I developed equipment to face the world as
an adult. Even now the adult part of me is watching
over the child part, that part which needs this dialogue with you and is hoping to hear from you soon.

Love,
Xenia

LEONARD'S ANSWER

Dear Xenia,

I was thrilled by your letter. Forgive me if I say I told you so. My timing was off when I suggested to you that you would have another major relationship, but my rationale for saying it was perfect. You are a woman who is good at relationships; a woman with a great deal to give and to get; someone who likes being married. Yes, you *can* be alone. You have proved it, but as your Warren once asked, "Why would you want to?"

I hardly recognized you in your last letters. You clearly were in a great deal of pain, which made you defensive and uncharacteristically dogmatic. You ranted and raved about wanting to be alone! You never acknowledged your joy when you found yourself sharing both your space and various hidden parts of you. How come you never mentioned the delight you felt when you walked into your apartment after a long day's work to find Warren comfortably in the kitchen organizing dinner? Wasn't that one of your first of many hidden reactions to the warmth and love—yes, love—that you wanted? And how about the internal glow you experienced at the sound of his razor and other signs that you were not living alone?

Well, you've put up quite a struggle against Warren's love for you and your love for him. I think I understand your fear about a second major loss. Anyone who has suffered the kind of pain that comes with loss will understand how vulnerable you feel. But you're someone who knows how to live and knows that loss is a part of living. You've pulled yourself up out of the dark pit and into a glorious bright life which now demands to be explored.

Of course you could be making a mistake if you remarry. Anyone making a serious decision is taking a risk. But what are the options? You could climb into bed and pull the covers over your head and hide. You could let your fear of failure destroy a relationship, one in which two well-matched people can grow and flourish. But you could also be your gutsy, courageous self whom I cherished for twenty years.

Now consider if the situation had been reversed. I know I would have wanted to remarry. I couldn't have stayed locked in a relationship that existed solely in my head. I would've felt stuck. Talk about doors, how ironic that you see an open door. I see our *us* part as a closed door shutting you in. Don't let it! You must find a way to let go totally so you can be free to live *your* life, not *ours*.

You know, you've changed a great deal. You've grown stronger and a lot healthier. You appear to be more fun and more of a risk-taker. My answer to your letter is—go for it! If it's my permission you need, I give it unconditionally, to the limit, and with my blessings. With the permission goes my love.

Leonard

Remarriage Does Not Mean Replacement

My widowed friends and I spent long hours grappling with the concept of replacement. Remarriage equaled replacement and replacement felt like the ultimate betrayal. How could anyone replace our late spouse? And if it were possible, what would it say about the lost spouse, us, our marriages?

"Peter knew me like a book," Sybil said. "I would be thinking about something and before I could open my mouth, Peter would say it!" Vera said, "Larry was my alter ego. How could anyone know me the way he did?"

I was silent, wondering if Leonard, with his infinite understanding of me, had always had his intuitive grasp of me and my mercurial moods or if he had learned it by living with me for so many years. Was it fair of us to be comparing a hypothetical new spouse with our lost loves who had spent years learning the language of our marriages?

Nevertheless, built into our concerns was that constant whisper of comparison. How could so-and-so possibly consider a man who was less brilliant or less amusing or less talented than her husband had been? How could anyone ever follow in anyone else's shoes?

My friend Jo Ann, previously an articulate proponent of the "never remarry" school, met Jack and consented to marry him. Excited and happy, she introduced him to her friends. I thought I already knew him, but we'd never met before. I saw him several times before I realized why he had seemed so familiar: he was a carbon copy of Jo Ann's first husband, Ralph. He had the same mannerisms, wore similar clothes, and, like Ralph, was a lawyer. Jo Ann said she felt as if she'd come home, that everything seemed so comfortable with Jack.

It stayed comfortable for her as long as Jack continued to remind her of Ralph. But one day he came to dinner in a bright red shirt. Jo Ann commented that Ralph wouldn't have been caught dead in a shirt like that. Jack, preferring compatibility to confrontation, remained silent. A week later Jo Ann told Jack his office looked too informal for a lawyer of his stature and proposed that he redecorate with a contemporary window treatment and more prestigious furniture. Jack thanked her for her interest and then gently suggested she let his workplace meet his needs and that perhaps it would be better if she did not interfere. Ralph had always taken her advice, and Jo Ann became increasingly anxious as Jack held to his position. Soon they fell to quarreling.

Jo Ann wanted an exact replica of Ralph, but Jack, despite the similarities, was different in many ways. As Jo Ann pushed to make him more like Ralph, he resisted, wanting to be cherished for his own qualities and not for those qualities that reminded Jo Ann of Ralph. It soon became clear that Jo Ann was not ready for a new relationship. When they broke up, Jack confessed that he had felt like a pale imitation of Ralph, with whom he could not compete. "Everyone knows," he said, "a copy never equals the original."

I've known other widows who made the same mistake because of their determination to replace, repeat, and reproduce their former relationships. Lois, attempting to find the life she had lived with her late husband, a doctor who traveled throughout the world being wined and dined, remarried an actor whom she assumed would offer her the same celebrity status. She failed to consider the fact that her husband, in addition to sharing his position with her, had also been a loving, considerate, connected, and caring man. Her new husband had equal celebrity status but was an abusive, combative, and demanding mate to whom she could not stay married.

I can predict trouble when I hear certain sentences: "He reminds me of my late . . .," "How could he be as good as . . .," and one of the most potentially destructive phrases, "How could anyone replace my . . ."

The dictionary defines replacement as "that which takes the place of anything discarded, worn out, or obsolete," or "one who takes the place of someone or something; a substitute." How can we widows think about our past loves in these terms? It's impossible to imagine how the word "replacement" became cemented in our thoughts, vocabularies, and actions. We lost someone; we didn't discard something that wore out. How can anyone take the place of a person with whom we began our life, grew, developed, changed, and with whom we created a shared world? There is no replacement either for him or for the part of us that is gone. What there is, however, is the new and the different.

Many widows have told me that if their husbands could see them in their new postmourning lives, see their growth, development, and self-confidence, they might not like the changes. Also, some widows, finding themselves so changed, wonder if they would choose the same kind of marriage as the one they had before.

Trudy, having been widowed for two years, told me that if she were to remarry she would look for a totally different life-style from the one that she had relished during her marriage. Both Trudy and Max, her husband, had been workaholics, but Trudy had recently learned to appreciate other aspects of her life. She now enjoyed her children and grandchildren in a way that she previously had not, and she found herself cutting back on her work schedule so that she could travel more, something she had always hoped to do.

Trudy told me about a man she had met while she was buying a hot dog from a street vendor. He told Trudy that she looked exactly like a 1940s movie star and suggested they take a walk in the park. Trudy said she couldn't think of a reason to say no, and off she went with him. She found herself laughing throughout the walk because Ken, her hot-dog companion, was so funny. Ken was a poet and a part-time librarian and told her that a daily stroll in the park was a requisite for maneuvering through life. He entertained her with stories about his travels and his joy at meeting new people.

Trudy was fascinated by her new friend, who was totally different from Max but equally compelling. She admitted that although he might not turn out to be the right man for her, he was a type of man that she could now find very attractive. "He's kind of what I'm about in my present incarnation," she said.

The phrase "present incarnation" hit me with a tremendous impact. Incarnation, renaissance, rebirth—everything new, a time to start again. Trudy was a new person in a different time in her life and not a young girl considering marriage within the old framework. She was Trudy, thirty years later, having already lived an entire first life and now ready for her next life. She would use parts of her first life, including her love for Max, to guide her through her future life.

I felt very much like Trudy: Warren and I were also reborn and starting again, each of us marrying someone different from our first spouse. Sometimes we played a game called "Would you have married me all those years ago? And would it have worked then?" We never could find answers because they were buried deep beneath our past lives.

However, I did find the answer to the replacement dilemma: no one had been replaced. Both Leonard and Belle (Warren's first wife) became a part of Warren's and my life together as we grew stronger and richer, closer and more loving. Each of them is still a part of us.

Now That You Know so Much,
Could You Make It Even Better?

Vera, saying she needed to devote all her time to running her business, had been the first one to leave our group. We were sorry to see her go, recognizing that her departure marked the beginning of the group's termination. I had resisted leaving despite my awareness that it was time to say good-bye. I hated to see it end; it had been my anchor and my refuge. Never having missed a meeting, I felt as if I had been at the core of our growth and changes as we worked our way through mourning, allowing one another to be our best and worst selves.

As I said my good-byes, the group began reminiscing about our first meeting. Sybil, Vera, Betsy, Norman, Cliff, and I agreed that at the time convalescing had seemed like an impossible task. But in the end we had found that each of us had a unique struggle and that each of our solutions had helped the others find their solutions.

We agreed that we would meet four more times and then disband. Norman's parting words stayed with me: "Listen, Blondie, wherever you are, whatever you're doing, don't forget 'the promise.' "

How could I forget a promise to never again take anything for granted? Before Leonard died I had been living as if our lives lasted forever. Of course I was prepared for some changes, predicting minor ill health, career changes, financial changes, perhaps a move—but we, Leonard and I, were forever. Unthreatened and childishly greedy, I thought of us as my entitlement.

I also took miracles for granted: someone to talk to late at night; someone to care for and someone who takes care of you in return; shared successes and failures; the unbroken connection with a love. I had never questioned the miracle of waking up in the morning and finding the world exactly the way it had been the day before. One day had followed the next until a day I learned, in one split second, that Leonard and my world had been totally shattered.

Jill, a patient, told me that it took her a full year after her husband died to rid herself of the notion that each day would bring a new form of terror. Her life had been vital and complete until the day of the fire, from which her husband never recovered. At first she awakened each day in a panic, expecting another disaster. But slowly, in time, she moved through her mourning to the days that she greeted with gratitude and pleasure, finally free of fear and pain. She would never again accept each day as if it were her due.

Like Jill, we in the group had promised never again to take our lives for granted, nor would we believe that our lives were ours for the asking or taking. We had learned to value each day, acknowledging its uniqueness.

Our promise had nothing to do with our early guilt—our "should-have," "could-have," "would-have" syndromes. Instead it was our statement about new definitions, new appreciations, and new knowledge for and about the important things in life.

Jill said her new set of values reminded her of her newest grandchild. Everything he did for the first time was applauded by those around him, marking it as a major event.

Feeling like a newborn dealing with her regenerated world, Jill now applauded each transaction, each sign of competency, each new friend, each new learning experience, all as if it were for the first time.

Madge, a patient, was another example of someone learning to value things differently; she too had started over. She moved to New York, began a career in fashion design, and was forced to make new friends. She described herself as "finally whole and integrated—grounded, like a fortress in my new world." She likened each of her transactions to a first meal after a lengthy period of deprivation, and as the first step on a healed leg after a bone had been broken. "Now that I know so much about life," she said, "I think I can make it even better."

I also knew much more. My internal devils that had plagued me for such a long time had finally disappeared. They had always been in my way making life far more complicated than it needed to be. Like Maggie I had been unparalleled at finding the negative in a situation, despite all its positive aspects. And like Maggie I was a pro at holding on to the negative, chewing it over like a dog with a bone.

The "Maggies" had gone and so had my tendency to act like them. I seemed far better able to see the positive and overlook the minor flaws in Warren's and my daily life. Learning to make things work had recently become a nourishing talent that served as a foundation for joy and love.

I was curious about my few widowed friends who had neither joined a group nor gone into individual therapy. They assured me that they hadn't needed outside support; their families and friends had offered them everything they had needed. When we compared our experiences, I noted once again the absence of set rules—different individuals find their own way, the way that works best for them. They had in common their deep connection to something or someone outside themselves.

We had all discovered that we would find opportunities that allowed us to give the best we had to offer. Dale, a patient, often spoke about her reverence for Eleanor Roosevelt, who, having lived in her husband's shadow, blossomed into one of the most important people in the world after her husband's death. Other widows used their unmarried status to allow them to do things they had never dared risk as part of a couple. Sandra, the quintessential suburban housewife, secretly had always wanted to learn to fly; she got her pilot's license a year after her husband died. Nora, previously terrified by the new and unfamiliar, studied Chinese for two years and got a position with an American company in China.

I know five widows who decided to buy a house together as an investment for their future. One of them explained, "I need to know I'll have a home when I'm old. This place will have enough room for at least four of us and, should we need them, caretakers. We will own all the shares and when one of us dies, the shares can only be sold to another widow."

Almost all my widowed friends were finding their way: working for the homeless, flying planes, taking care of AIDS victims. They were involved in new relationships, new careers, and new lives. None of us had chosen to start again, but having been forced to do so, we were surprising ourselves with our new capabilities.

Now that we knew so much more, we could make it better by cherishing each day, each relationship, and each new experience.

You too have options, alternatives, and choices to make. They are all out there, just waiting for the changed you to discover them.

Epilogue

Last night I dreamed about Leonard. Unlike my earlier dreams, it was a happy dream filled with beautiful lights and vibrant colors. It looked as if it were fall, my favorite time of year. Ever since I was a little girl I've associated fall with a new beginning—a new school year, with new friends and new challenges. Even the air seems fresh and new.

Leonard was dressed in a handsome dark wool suit, dressed for fall. He was carrying a suitcase and I felt very comfortable talking to him about his travels. Nothing seemed odd or peculiar. He knew everything about me. We talked about Warren and how wonderful it was that we were to be married at the end of the month. Leonard and I reviewed the years of my struggle without him—how my despair had actually changed my personality, leaving me empty and joyless.

Leonard smiled knowingly as I attempted to describe the changes that had taken place between me and the friends he and I had once shared. He listened as I explained other changes in my life.

"More," he said. "Tell me more about you and Warren."

I told him that I had never felt so totally at peace with myself; I no longer needed to punch my way through each day. I attributed these feelings to living with Warren, who had taught me that life would be there whether I punched it or not.

I could see approval in Leonard's eyes as I continued. It was important to me to tell him that he had made a major contribution to my capability to remarry. I had learned how to be married from him and although I had been a reluctant student, he was, as always, a master teacher.

He patted my cheek in a familiar gesture, saying, "You've come back. You've come back to your loving self." He seemed incredibly happy and tranquil as he picked up his suitcase, turned once more to wave, and was gone.

Index

Xenia Rose, M.A., C.S.W., was born in New York City and received degrees from Sarah Lawrence College, New York University, and Columbia University. She was the administrative director of psychiatric services at the Westchester Health Maintenance Organization before becoming director of outpatient services at Four Winds Hospital in Katonah, New York.

Xenia Rose has been in full-time private practice since 1979 and lives in New York City with her husband, documentary filmmaker and writer, Warren Forma.